# THE STORY OF SOCIETY'S FAVOURITE STORE

EBURY PRESS
LONDON

ACKNOWLEDGMENTS

I would like to thank Nadene Hansen of the Harrods Archives, whose help was invaluable in researching this book, David Wilkinson of the Books department and Marguerite Patten for her kind help. Alison Wormleighton deserves the credit for devising the structure of the book as well as editing the text, and Gillian Haslam for making it happen.

First published by Ebury Press
an imprint of the Random Century Group
Random Century House, 20 Vauxhall Bridge Road
London SW1V 2SA

British Library Cataloguing in Publication Data
Callery, Sean
    Harrods: the story of society's favourite store.
    1. London. (London Borough) Kensington and Chelsea.
    Department stores. Harrods, history
    I. Title
    381.14106542134
    ISBN 0-85223-989-0

Edited by Alison Wormleighton
Designed by Harry Green
Picture Research by Lynda Marshall

Filmset in Monotype Baskerville by Advanced Filmsetters (Glasgow) Limited
Printed and bound in Italy by New Interlitho S.p.a., Milan

# CONTENTS

# FOREWORD

BY THE CHAIRMAN OF HARRODS LIMITED,
MR. MOHAMED AL FAYED

Harrods started life in the middle of the nineteenth century around the time of The Great Exhibition in Hyde Park, which brought visitors from all over the world to a little known and somewhat insalubrious village called Knightsbridge. Harrods began as a family firm and so it is once more. When my brothers and I acquired the company in 1985, we knew that we had bought more than a store. Here was a legend, a British institution with a special place in the hearts of many people, in England and throughout the world.

Two families, the Harrods and then the Burbidges, laid the foundations of the business and built upon those foundations by doing one simple thing supremely well. They put the customer first. By anticipating their customers' wishes, and serving them with courtesy and skill, they established a name which is unrivalled in the world. My family and I are dedicated to continuing their traditions of innovation and excellence.

As we approach the twenty-first century, the store has grown beyond the wildest ambitions of its founders. A constant process of expansion is helping to make Harrods the largest store in the world while an extensive refurbishment programme is restoring much of the store to its legendary Edwardian opulence.

This book draws together many strands of the story of Harrods – its customers, its staff, its place in society and its role in time of war, the regular emergence of new departments, and the fascinating and always changing picture of a building evolving through this century.

As you turn the pages, you will find details of the many elements which contribute to the legend of Harrods – the famous terracotta frontage, the

distinctive green carrier bags, the spectacular Food Halls, and the Green Men who are to the world at large the face of Harrods.

Unlike nearly all department stores, which began as drapers' shops, Harrods started as a grocery and the Food Halls are still the heart of the business. That is one of the reasons why I make it a point to get into my white coat and straw boater in order to serve behind the counter as often as possible. The founders of Harrods became successful because they never lost touch with the store's customers. What was right for them is certainly right for me.

I find it inspiring to see how Harrods has stayed at the forefront of retailing and customer service for so long and in so many ways. When the present building was erected, its grandeur took people's breath away. That happened, literally, when Harrods installed London's first escalator in the late nineteenth century. The management were so concerned that customers would be overcome by the excitement of riding upon it that a butler was stationed at the head of the escalator to administer calming brandy or reviving smelling salts, according to taste. People have now become accustomed to the 'moving stairs' but it is my belief that the element of excitement in visiting a great store must never be lost.

If we do not make sure that shopping is a pleasure and that service is as good as it can possibly be, we do not deserve to succeed. I am resolved that Harrods will be worthy of its past and equal to the challenges of the future. Within these covers, you will find the story of our traditions and our heritage which make up the very fabric of the store. Here is Harrods' past and present, but bear in mind that we are still writing the future chapters of a story which combines all the elements of drama and glamour. Don't let anyone ever tell you business is boring – here is the romance of retailing.

OPPOSITE: The illuminated Harrods building, with its four royal warrants in pride of place. On this occasion, the Danish flag is flying in honour of a visit by Queen Margrethe of Denmark.

Telegrams, Everything London.
Telephone, 542.995 Kensington.
„ 638 Westminster.

# Harrod's Ltd

## FREE TO ALL

LIST OF DEPARTMENTS

ANTIQUE FURNITURE.
ART NEEDLEWORK.
BAKERY.
BANKING.
BEERS & MINERAL WATERS.
BOOKS, BOOKBINDING.
BOOTS.
BOYS' CLOTHING.
BRUSHES.
BUILDING & DECORATING.
CABINETS & BEDDING.
CARRIAGES (HIRE OF).
CAMP & MILITARY EQUIPMENT.
CATERING.
CARPETS & LINOLEUMS.
CHILDREN'S COSTUMES.
CHINA & GLASS.
CIGARS & TOBACCOS.
COALS.
CONFECTIONERY.
COOKED MEATS.
CUTLERY.
CYCLES & SPORTS.
DRAPERY.
DRESS MATERIALS.
DRESS MAKING.
DRUGS & PERFUMERY.
DISPENSING.
DYEING & CLEANING.
ELECTRICAL ENGINEERING.
FEATHERS & ARTIFICIAL FLOWERS.
FISH.
FLOWERS & PLANTS.
FORAGE.
FOREIGN EXPRESS (PARCELS).
FRUIT & VEGETABLE.
FURNISHING DRAPERY & BLINDS.
FURNITURE.
FURS.
GARDEN FURNITURE.
GLOVES.
GROCERY.
HABERDASHERY.
HAIR-DRESSING SALOON.
HARNESS & SADDLERY.

LIST OF DEPARTMENTS

HATS.
HIRE & ENTERTAINMENTS.
HOSIERY.
HOUSE & ESTATE AGENCY.
INSURANCE—LIFE, FIRE, BURGLARY, &c.
IRONMONGERY.
JEWELLERY & PLATE.
LACE & FANCY GOODS.
LACE CURTAINS.
LADIES' UNDERCLOTHING.
LAMPS.
LIVERY STABLES.
MANICURE.
MEAT.
MILLINERY.
MUSIC.
OPTICAL.
ORIENTAL.
OUTFITTING.
PHOTOGRAPHY.
PIANOS, &c.
PICTURES.
POULTRY & GAME.
PRINTS & CALICOES.
PROVISIONS.
RAILWAY & STEAMSHIP BOOKING OFFICE.
REMOVALS & WAREHOUSING.
RESTAURANT & DINING HALL.
RIBBONS.
SEEDS, BULBS, &c.
SILKS & VELVETS.
SAFE DEPOSIT.
STATIONERY.
STOCK & SHARE BROKERS.
TEA GOWNS.
TAILORING.
THEATRE TICKETS.
TOYS & GAMES.
TRIMMINGS.
TRUNKS.
TURNERY.
UMBRELLAS.
WATERPROOF GOODS.
WINES & SPIRITS.
WOOLS.

Elevation of Premises in Brompton Road.

## The most fashionable resort FOR SHOPPING IN LONDON

### HANDSOMELY ILLUSTRATED CATALOGUE
THE BEST EVER ISSUED
AND
EXCEEDING 1000 PAGES
Obtainable upon Application

## EVERYTHING FOR EVERYBODY

## HARRODS LIMITED, BROMPTON ROAD, LONDON.
✳ ✳ ✳ ✳ ✳ ✳ ✳  Managing Director, RICHARD BURBRIDGE.

# CHAPTER ONE

# AN INTRODUCTION TO THE STORE

*Harrods*

# "An Institution of much Interest and Beauty"

In 1913 the head of the Postal department at Harrods boasted: 'It is an axiom in international postal circles that only two types of letters with insufficient address are delivered without being referred to the "Blind Department": they are letters addressed to "The King, England" and "The Pope, Rome". We have added to this list by receiving a letter addressed to Harrods Stores, England.' By the time at which he was speaking, Harrods had firmly established itself as the most prestigious store in the world. It still holds that position today: utter the name 'Harrods' anywhere on the globe, and eyes will light up with recognition. People from all over the world visit the store in vast numbers, not only to shop but for the experience itself.

Harrods has become an institution: the 'top people's store', the local shop for nearby Buckingham Palace, the place to go for the best in quality and service. It is a reputation Harrods forged early in the twentieth century, at a time when competition between stores was intensifying by the day. Perhaps more remarkable has been its achievement in maintaining, even polishing up, that sparkling image over the subsequent decades. The store has retained its reputation by keeping up with retailing trends, by continuing to offer a huge range of goods and services, and by setting a

OPPOSITE: A full-page advertisement from the 1902 Coronation issue of *The Sketch*. It lists ninety-one departments at the store, from antique furniture to wools.

consistently high standard of service to its customers, who include the upper crust of society.

## TRANSFORMATION OF A VICTORIAN GROCERY STORE

One of the ironies of the Harrods story is that the family whose name appears in lights on its edifice as the beacon of exclusivity in London did little to create the giant that is Harrods today. Charles Henry Harrod, founder of the store, had taken over a small grocer's shop in the 1840s, in what was then an insalubrious outpost on the edge of town. His son, Charles Digby Harrod, built the store up to a decent size by the time of his retirement in 1889, when Harrods was formed into a limited company. But it was three generations of the Burbidge family which formed the dynasty that pushed Harrods ahead of the field and transformed it from a modest emporium into one of the largest shops in the world. The Burbidge family ran the store for seventy years.

The foundations of Harrods' greatness were set in place during the reign of the first Burbidge, Richard (later Sir Richard). In 1890 Harrods was an ailing company employing 200 staff and making a profit of £13,519. Burbidge joined the next year, and within two decades profits had risen more than tenfold and the staff numbered 6,000. Harrods had become the largest department store in London. It was renowned the world over, and the wealthiest people on the globe wanted to shop there. The store adopted

This 1891 bill for 'filling window boxes and man's time' shows the store diversifying into home services – it also offered clock-winding in local houses for many years.

the telegraphic address 'Everything, London', reflecting its status as the emporium from which even the most unlikely goods were available. It also devised a motto, 'Omnia, Omnibus, Ubique' (Everything for Everybody Everywhere), which it has succeeded in living up to.

The reputation was worldwide. For example, a woman from a very well-bred family recalled of her Edwardian childhood: 'When we were children and lived in the South of France, our nurse was known as Harrods, because she could always produce whatever anybody needed.' Actress Dame Sybil Thorndike, interviewed on tour in Calcutta, was asked her religion. 'Church of England,' she replied. 'Oh, like Harrods,' came the response, 'your religion supplies everything for everybody.'

## DYNAMISM AND VISION

Richard Burbidge was a teetotal, non-smoking workaholic, who succeeded in blending the zest of a visionary with the opportunism of an entrepreneur. Familiar with the development of department stores in America, he had the foresight and determination gradually to buy up the entire island site that Harrods occupies today. He made sure that his staff provided the kind of service that impressed even the most haughty aristocrat, and rewarded them with the best conditions of employment in the retail trade at the time.

Burbidge even spent his holidays gathering ideas from overseas. When doctors told him in 1911 to take the longest sea journey he could find,

HARRODS LTD. LONDON, S.W. *The most elegant & commodious EMPORIUM in the WORLD.*

A postcard from 1910 showing a somewhat idealised version of the Harrods frontage.
The store has never been slow to publicise itself with such devices.

before he wore himself out, it merely prompted another burst of dynamism. After drumming his fingers all the way to South America, he spent five days in Buenos Aires, and cabled back to his board that the city was so prosperous it was going to be the 'Paris of the West' and Harrods should open a store there. The result, in 1913, was the cutting of the ribbon at Harrods (Buenos Aires) and the beginning of the Harrods Group. (The store is still trading although it has no link with Harrods today.) Burbidge injected so much energy and imagination into his job that he died exhausted in 1917 when he should have been enjoying the warm glow of satisfaction of his baronetcy while his son Sir Woodman continued the good work as managing director.

Sir Woodman Burbidge inherited his father's drive but adopted a rather more aristocratic air. He began building the Harrods Group with acquisitions of stores such as London's Dickins & Jones and Swan & Edgar. (Swan & Edgar was later resold.) He led the flagship store through some tough times in the 1920s and 1930s, cutting staff and acquisitions when it was imperative, and polishing the sense of pride the store had developed.

## THE 'SECRET OF HARRODS'

In 1924 Sir Woodman wrote: 'Hive, as Harrods is, of thousands of busy hands and brains, home of countless differing elements, focus of every type of temperament, Harrods has somehow so unified itself, so co-ordinated its manifold elements, so collaborated and co-operated in the pursuance of clear-cut aims, ideals and policies, that it has become almost like some

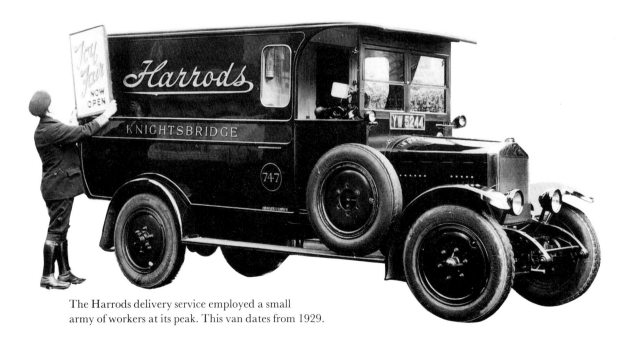

The Harrods delivery service employed a small
army of workers at its peak. This van dates from 1929.

astounding superman, gifted with powers unparalleled, brimming with personality, the very essence and embodiment of interest.' This 'interest', he believed, was 'the secret of Harrods'. Sir Woodman was not just running a shop by now. The staff included architects, boxmakers, cycle repairers, dispensers, engravers, furriers, jewellers, lace workers, milliners, opticians, printers, sausage makers, tea blenders, upholsterers and watchmakers: almost an A–Z of light industry! Profits topped half a million pounds in 1920 (the year the company changed its name to 'Harrods Ltd'), and although the store had to struggle to maintain its high level of trade during the tough periods of the decade, profits nevertheless rose.

In 1935 Sir Woodman's son Richard – 'Mr Richard' to the staff before he inherited the title – assumed the mantle of responsibility and continued with the philosophy of blending quality goods with excellent service. He also worked within the family tradition of shrewd business practice tempered by patriarchal concern for the staff (Mr Richard's memory for the names of his employees was legendary).

In 1949 the store celebrated its centenary. A special insert in the Daily Mail noted that in addition to the array of goods it offered as a department store, Harrods held nearly two million pounds of customers' money in current accounts at its own bank, lent a million books a year from its library, and was holding almost half a million pounds' worth of furs in its cold storage rooms. It was very obvious that the store was actually succeeding in being 'Everything, London'!

## CHANGING TIMES

Society after World War II, however, was very different from the regimented class system of earlier years. A new middle class had grown up that appreciated quality but did not require it served up on a silver platter by a liveried servant. The world inhabited by Harrods – the store which had catered for the needs and whims of gentility for decades – was changing dramatically. Counter service was giving way to self service, customisation to mass production. Sir Richard Burbidge, who possessed his father's and grandfather's charm as well as their capacity for hard work, was faced with a difficult challenge. Harrods, traditionally the pace-setter, the store that pioneered innovations, had to meet its customers' new requirements without sacrificing its high standards of quality and service.

## THE JEWEL IN THE CROWN

Despite a fall in profits in real terms, Harrods retained its formidable reputation. The Harrods Group continued to grow, and by 1959 Harrods was the jewel in the crown of a group of eight stores, the others being Dickins & Jones and DH Evans in London, Rackhams in Birmingham, Kendal Milne in Manchester, Hendersons in Liverpool, John Walsh of Sheffield and JF Rockhey in the West Country. Together they formed the fifth-largest department store chain in Great Britain. The group's properties were revalued at £20 million, and on issued capital of £8 million, that made it vulnerable to a takeover bid.

Richard Burbidge was aware of the prospect and approached the largest store group in the land, Debenhams, inviting a purchase. It was not to be so simple: 1959 saw the Harrods Group as the celebrated target for a three-cornered fight involving Debenhams; the House of Fraser, a Scottish drapery group led by Hugh Fraser (later Lord Fraser); and United Drapery Stores. Amid speculation and rumour the trio battled in public and behind the scenes for control of the famous store, until Joseph Collier of United Drapery Stores decided to withdraw and sold his shares to Hugh Fraser. After a well-orchestrated campaign, Fraser attended his first board meeting as the chairman of Harrods, in September 1959. The Harrods Group was now part of the House of Fraser.

## MAJOR INNOVATIONS

The store reinforced its pioneering image in the 1960s with the opening of the innovative boutique, Way In. Essentially a shop within a shop (it began

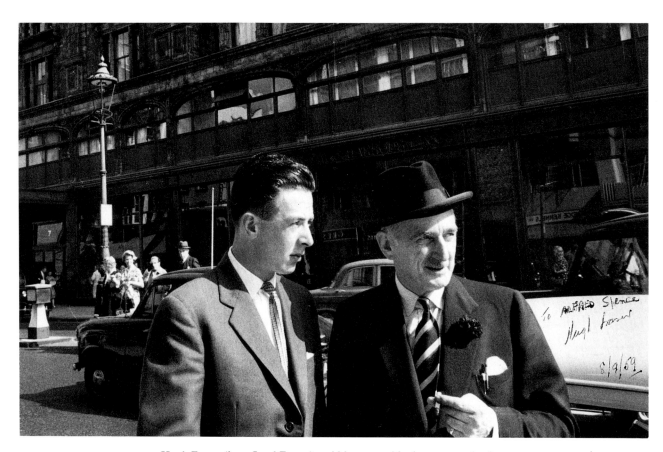

Hugh Fraser (later Lord Fraser) and his son outside the store on the day
their company acquired the Harrods Group in September 1959.

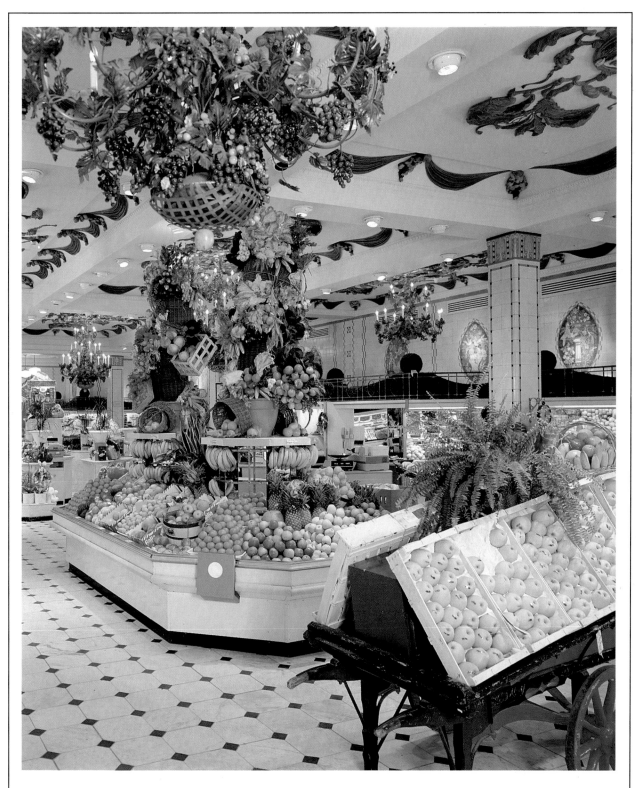

The refurbished Fruit and Vegetables Hall, its spectacular ceilings
complementing the colourful displays of produce below. This restoration to
its former glory was part of a massive investment in the store in the 1980s.

life as a separate company), Way In was one of the top boutiques in London for almost a decade.

In 1966 Lord Hugh Fraser died and was succeeded by his son, Sir Hugh Fraser. Then, in 1970, the arrival of the visionary managing director Robert Midgley brought about a major transformation of Harrods. Midgley saw that the huge Banking Hall was taking up valuable selling space on the ground floor, and that the workrooms in the Trevor Square building, where Harrods was still churning out its own chocolate, bread, tailoring, silverwork and other quality craftwork, were out-of-date. He cut them, ruthlessly, unpopularly, and rightly.

Midgley put Harrods back on track despite the recession in the early 1970s. He was helped by a dramatic rise in the number of tourists (who had a visit to Harrods listed on their itineraries next to Buckingham Palace and Madame Tussaud's), and by the influx of oil-rich Arab customers. As the 1970s became the 1980s, Harrods was itself a boomtown, with turnover, profits and even the salesfloor growing as the management invested in improving the premises.

## CHANGE OF OWNERSHIP

The ten years from the second half of the 1970s were less happy times in the board room. Sir Hugh Fraser, winner of the 'Young Businessman of the Year' award in 1973, was deposed as chairman by Professor Roland Smith in 1981.

By this time longstanding shareholder Lonrho, headed by 'Tiny' Rowland, had already tried and failed in a bid for the whole group, suggesting in one proposal that it could be better run as a set of separate, 'demerged' stores, and amassing a 29.9 per cent stake in the group. A hostile full bid in early 1981 was stalled by a reference to the Monopolies Commission, and Lonrho agreed not to repeat its bid without the permission of the Department of Trade (later Department of Trade and Industry).

After years of negotiation with the Monopolies Commission and the Department of Trade and Industry, Lonrho sold its shares in the House of Fraser to Alfayed Investment and Trust (UK) PLC in October 1984. Lonrho immediately began building a new stake of 6.4 per cent in the House of Fraser.

In March 1985 Alfayed Investment and Trust (UK) PLC made a cash offer for the remaining equity of the group, which was accepted. For a total of £615 million, the three Fayed brothers, Mohamed Al Fayed, Ali Fayed and Salah Fayed had taken over the House of Fraser and its flagship Harrods store. Mohamed Al Fayed had been doing business in the UK for more than thirty years, with interests including the construction and civil engineering industries, and oil trading. In 1979 he had purchased the Paris Ritz Hotel – a French national institution on a par with Harrods in

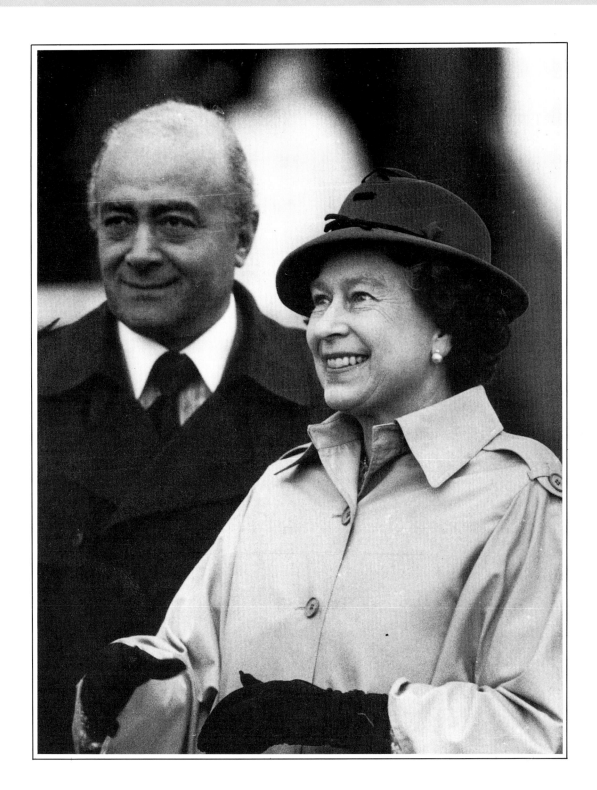

Harrods' chairman Mohamed Al Fayed with Her Majesty the Queen.

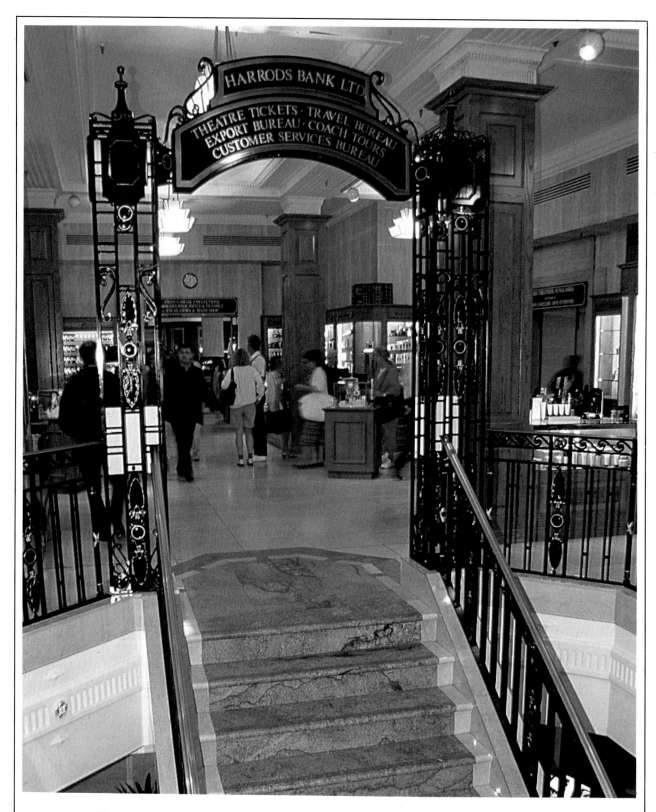

The impressive ground-floor entrance to the new Harrods Bank, which was re-established in 1989 in the basement of the building. The opening up of the basement for retail use is another landmark in the store's development.

The fixtures and fittings of the new Harrods Bank were based on the original
architect's drawings, to recreate the elegance of the Edwardian era.

Britain – and spent $150 million in restoring it to its former glory.
Following accusations by Lonrho, the Department of Trade and Industry
conducted an investigation into the purchase of the House of Fraser, but no
further action was taken by the government.

### BACK TO HARRODS' ROOTS

Mohamed Al Fayed became chairman of Harrods, which reverted to
private company status in 1986. He takes a keen and constant interest in
every aspect of the business, from the shop floor to the major building work
commenced in the late 1980s. In a sense, under Mohamed Al Fayed,
Harrods has gone back to its roots as a private concern with its proprietor
keeping an attentive eye on its activities.

Still Harrods continues to expand and to adapt, meeting the needs of a
changing, increasingly international clientele. The store today has about
300 departments and is visited by 35,000 customers a day. Its famous Sales
are regarded as the perfect time to pick up a bargain, yet it retains its image
of exclusivity, of being the 'top people's store' – even when it is crammed
with customers struggling to find their way round its labyrinthine layout. A
visit to Harrods is a must for any visitor to the capital, but it is not merely a
tourist attraction: the store continues to provide its customers with the best
in service and quality. The telegram may have faded into history, but the
'Everything, London' tag has stayed in place.

The bluff features of Charles Henry Harrod,
miller turned wholesaler turned grocer, who founded
the store in the mid-nineteenth century

# CHAPTER TWO

# THE FIRST SIXTY YEARS

*Harrods*

# "A Reputation for Quality"

During its formative years, Harrods developed from a struggling grocery shop into 'the world's greatest emporium', as it described itself around the time of its sixtieth anniversary.

The man whose name adorns Harrods would have been amazed that his humble grocer's evolved into anything more than a simple, honest shop, let alone a huge department store. Stocky and broad-shouldered, Charles Henry Harrod looked like that archetypical Englishman John Bull. He was a careful man of limited ambition – certainly no retailing visionary. Born in 1800, he was a miller in Clacton, Essex, before he began supplying tea and some other groceries (wholesale and retail) from a shop in Stepney, east London, in 1834. He married Elizabeth Digby, daughter of a local pork butcher, and they produced three sons. One of his customers, who became a friend, was Philip Henry Burden. Burden ran a small grocer's shop in Knightsbridge, which was then a rather run-down, insalubrious area on the western fringes of London.

### THE DEVELOPMENT OF KNIGHTSBRIDGE

The hamlet of Knesbyrig is mentioned in a charter of King Edward the Confessor in the eleventh century. The land was leased to Westminster Abbey, which the king founded. It is likely that he had a bridge built over the West Bourne river near the present Albert Gate in Hyde Park, one of the Royal Parks. A couple of centuries on, the village name had evolved into Knyghtebrigge. One of the more fanciful legends that grew up about the name is that it commemorates two knights on their way to the Crusades who fought each other on the bridge. However, it is more likely that the name evolved from the word 'neat', meaning cattle, and referring to a time when beasts would be slaughtered at the hamlet before being taken on a few miles for sale in London.

The village was a haven in times of plague and illness, the great diarist Samuel Pepys picnicking there in 1666. The naming of nearby Constitution Hill testifies to the area's reputation as a health resort. During the eighteenth century it sported a gallows (and dispensation for the locals to keep the possessions of those who were strung up on them), and was a popular destination for families escaping the grime of London. At this time neighbouring Belgravia was largely an open space called Five Fields, and was the scene of many duels.

By the middle of the nineteenth century, Knightsbridge had become an unsavoury neighbourhood on the way from London to Kensington. Its maze of dark alleyways contrasted markedly with the wider streets of Belgravia, which was by that time more developed and salubrious. At night the shadowy, narrow streets of Knightsbridge were places of danger, haunted by robbers who worked in pairs: one would stalk the victim from behind and stretch a cord across his neck, while his accomplice emptied the helpless stranger's pockets. Barracks had been put up nearby, and residents were sufficiently annoyed by the noise of the soldiers that they petitioned (unsuccessfully) for the removal of these establishments.

## BURDEN'S SHOP

This was the setting for Burden's grocery store, at 8 Middle Queen's Buildings, which Charles Harrod was to take over in the mid-nineteenth century. Flanked by a stationer's and a brush shop, it was in the middle of a terrace of two-storey houses whose front gardens had been built over to create a row of small, flat-roofed shops. The premises were in good repair, having been built as recently as 1840. The shop had a turnover of about £20 per week from goods such as soap, biscuits, candles and tea, sold from one counter at the centre of its sawdust-covered floor. Nearby were two other grocers – Jobbins, across the passage, and John Barnes a few doors away – creating a bustling environment filled with the noise of shop-keepers barking out the merits of their wares.

Burden was in financial difficulties, and his astute supplier Harrod helped out, meeting the rent demands and not pushing for repayments. As the hapless grocer continued to struggle, Harrod became more involved in running the business. He was particularly concerned that Burden would emigrate to escape his debts, leaving Harrod with nothing to show for his effort and expenditure. In fact, Burden did eventually leave the country – which was probably just as well, as watching his shop develop into a major enterprise under someone else's ownership might have been rather galling!

The exact date when Harrod finally took over entirely is unclear. For many years it was accepted as 1849. Yet this was also the year when Harrod

An artist's impression of the humble grocery store at the time
that Charles Henry Harrod took it over.

opened his new outlet in the City at 38 Eastcheap. It is unlikely that a man
who was careful with money and was supporting a young family would
have simultaneously taken on a new challenge in the demanding retail
trade on the other side of London. The shop, which was open long hours,
required constant supervision. Another factor in Harrod's eventual
decision to move out from the congested city to Knightsbridge may have
been the London cholera epidemic of 1848/49, which claimed 13,000 lives.

Whatever the exact date of the final take-over, it can be assumed that
Harrod had played an increasingly important role in the shop for a number
of years. Perhaps he left Burden only nominally in charge from 1849. At
any rate, he had taken over every detail by 1853, when he began paying the

rates in his own name and moved his family into the house over the shop. The years on the sidelines, watching Burden make his mistakes, must have provided an invaluable apprenticeship for Charles Harrod in the business.

## A PROSPEROUS NEIGHBOURHOOD

Knightsbridge was changing. As London expanded, fuelled by the prosperity of the empire-building Victorians, the demand for space to build new houses pushed builders further afield. There was also a general exodus from the City, where commercial buildings were replacing many residences. The Great Exhibition of 1851 held in nearby Hyde Park introduced a new social cachet to the area, and opened up wide avenues which fostered the development of Kensington and Chelsea as residential neighbourhoods. It also funded the building of the South Kensington

The Great Exhibition of 1851 was held in Hyde Park and attracted countless visitors to the previously unfashionable area around Knightsbridge.

Museum (later the Victoria and Albert Museum) in 1857. Queen Victoria put the place firmly on the society map when she attended a costume ball at the nearby French Embassy in May 1854.

The growing wealth of Knightsbridge meant that the area could support a number of grocers. Partly for this reason and partly by virtue of sheer hard work, Charles Harrod was able to rescue the shop from its poor performance. He and his two assistants were at the store throughout its opening hours of 8am to 11pm. Harrod changed the shop very little during his time in charge. He did not even install a door to his house; entry remained via the shop front itself. He relied for business mainly on sales of tea over the counter. Perhaps he felt he had done enough through his success as a miller, then as a trader in the City, and now as a shopowner in an increasingly prosperous neighbourhood.

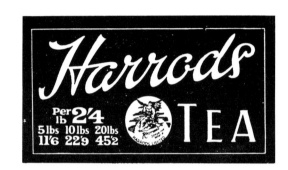

Tea is one of the staples the store has sold ever since its earliest days. This advertisement dates from 1929.

## A PREFERENCE FOR HARD CASH

Elizabeth Harrod died in 1860, by which time the shopowner was sixty himself and had already outlasted the then average life expectancy of forty-one years. (Only 7.2 per cent of men lived beyond that age at this time.) The following year he decided to retire. One of his sons, Charles Digby, who was born in 1841, had been apprenticed to a grocer in the City and had worked at the shop for some time. Now the stern father taught his twenty-year-old son an early business lesson: instead of handing over the shop, he offered to let him buy it for, it is believed, £500. The preference for hard cash was to be echoed nearly thirty years later by Charles Digby himself, who insisted on being paid in cash when he sold the business and would not accept shares in the newly formed limited company.

A livelier soul than his father, Charles Digby Harrod was energetic and eager to get on. He agreed to pay his father for the business over a set number of years, and he is said to have formally sacked and re-engaged his two assistants as he took over control of the business, to make the point that he, and not his father, was now in control. For three years he concentrated on mastering his trade and building on existing custom. In 1864 he paid

Charles Digby Harrod, who took over the store from his father in the 1860s and was responsible for its early expansion.

the last instalment to his father, married his sweetheart Caroline Godsmark and set up house with her behind the shop (now re-designated as 105 Brompton Road). Secure in his ownership of a steady business, a dynamic twenty-three-year-old with a sound head for trade and the ability to spot an opportunity, Charles Digby stepped up a gear.

At that time there were very few large shops in London, certainly no department stores, and most retail outlets were very small affairs offering a limited range of exclusive items. The grocery trade worked on very different practices to those of today. Dependent on repeat custom from the local large, prosperous households, grocers were quite prepared to offer small bribes to the servants who came to purchase goods. In addition, retailers offered generous credit terms, sometimes up to several years. This allowed the servants to reclaim cash for expenditure which they would not actually have to part with for some time – a lucrative benefit. Naturally, it also pushed up prices. Yet, although bribery and extended credit were the order of the day, Harrod stopped both practices at his shop. It was a bold innovation at a time when even the most fashionable of grocers (among which Harrod's shop certainly did not number) were happy to 'play the game' – but Charles Digby Harrod had another gamble to take, too.

## PRICE CUTS AND PROMOTIONS

In the 1860s a major threat to the small independent grocers emerged with the southward march of the Co-operative movement. This grouped shops together to gain better prices by buying in bulk, and passed the savings on in the form of discount prices to its 'members' – shoppers prepared to join the movement themselves for a modest subscription. Harrod was in charge of premises which were far better than those the Co-operatives ran, but this was not enough, and he seized the challenge and cut his prices. Then he booked his first newspaper advertisement, in the *Pall Mall Gazette*, using the aggressive headline, 'Co-operative prices'. In fact, Harrod was the first grocer to take full-page newspaper advertisements. These bold moves, of dropping prices and experimenting with new forms of promotion, were a huge risk for a small-time family grocer.

The gamble worked. By early 1867 he was employing five assistants and had installed a new shop front and plate-glass window, decorated only with his name in gold letters on the wire blinds. To Charles Digby Harrod, window displays smacked of ostentation. By the end of the following year he was achieving turnover of £1,000 per week, and was established as the biggest grocer on the block.

## EARLY EXPANSION AND DIVERSIFICATION

Increasingly prosperous, the Harrod family moved from the house behind the shop to a house in Esher, Surrey, in 1868. Seven years later they moved to Sydenham, a respectable south London suburb close by the carefully reconstructed Crystal Palace that had first been erected in Hyde Park in 1851 for the Great Exhibition. Harrod commuted in by pony-and-trap from his suburban home to the store.

The old kitchen and parlour were now converted to storage areas, and the first floor formed extra selling space. Here, encouraged by his sixteen-year-old cousin William Kibble, who had now joined the firm (and was to stay all his working life), Harrod began to stock perfumes, stationery, and the popular patent medicines of the time at cut prices. These were put in a corner of the first floor to lead customers past displays of other goods. The first step towards the modern department store had been taken.

Part of a Harrods bill from 1878, complete with the stipulation that Mr Harrod would accept cash only and offered no credit, unlike his competitors.

The Crimean War of 1870 hurt many London businesses, but Charles was working from a firm base now, and that June he introduced a 65-page price catalogue. The first of many such publications, it offered 'Groceries, Italian Goods etc . . . at the lowest possible prices for Nett Cash'. A delivery service to local houses was available, since it was out of the question for respectable customers to take away their purchases themselves. In addition, goods could be ordered from anywhere in the land. The invoices carried a clear warning: 'Mr Harrod begs to mention that he sells *exclusively for cash*. All country orders *must be paid for* previous to their being despatched.' Every morning, decked out in his customary uniform of bowler hat and shirt-sleeves, he would welcome sixteen employees to the shop. He had a weekly wage bill of £15, which included ten shillings each to the two delivery boys who struggled through the cobbled streets with their heavy carts.

## A GROWING REPUTATION

During the decade of the 1870s the business boomed. The small back garden – last vestige of the building's original residential use – disappeared under a two-storey extension. The shop was further enlarged in 1874 with the acquisition of the leases on the adjacent premises at 101 and 103 Brompton Road, and the legend 'Harrod's Stores' appeared for the first time on the windows. There was now sufficient room to stock cooked meats, confectionery and china. By 1876 the business was making enough deliveries to allow the purchase of a horse and cart.

Harrod's Stores was gaining a reputation for quality as Kibble returned each morning from Covent Garden market with fruit and vegetables as good as those at the fashionable Piccadilly grocers such as Fortnum and Mason. In 1880 Harrod began selling own-label groceries, evidence of his faith in using the name as a guarantee of quality.

By 1880 Harrod had about 100 staff on his books, and he cajoled them along with a carrot and a stick. They received pay for overtime (unusual at the time) and a bonus of a sovereign on their annual holiday. Yet they could be sacked at a moment's notice, which happened on occasion, and

This mock-up of the early store was created
for the 1949 centenary celebrations. Mr Harrod is
weighing tea at the counter.

were fined a penny halfpenny for every fifteen minutes they were late. Harrod was a stern disciplinarian who inspired both love and fear in his staff, and his familiar cry as he bustled past was, 'No humbugging. Get on with it.' An office clerk, FW Weston, recalled that Harrod, though stern, could be generous. 'He was fairly tall, with a big round face, and a twinkle in his eye, that either would mean an increase of salary if he sent for you, or something worse.' He still served special customers himself and was known to fund the purchases of some who fell on hard times. 'Put it on my account, tell her it's a gift,' he would mutter.

## LATE-VICTORIAN KNIGHTSBRIDGE

The opening of the Natural History Museum in 1881, following upon the long-delayed opening of the Royal Albert Hall ten years before, enhanced the respectability of the area and attracted more passing trade. Harrod's Stores considered itself the aristocrat in the neighbourhood, but life in the village of Knightsbridge remained full of contrasts. Day-to-day life was improving, as London reaped the benefits of the great Victorian public health programmes. Better drainage, public baths, and streets that were swept regularly and lit by gas lamps, all made life more salubrious. Yet a clerk of the time wrote, 'I have never seen so much poverty as existed in the neighbourhood', adding that in some houses 'people were herded together like so many animals, and the street was a mass of filth from one end to the other.' He recalled that a large woodyard behind the store was 'overrun with rats, and often on Sundays gentlemen used to bring dogs and catch a great many of them.'

Local children loitered outside the shop, waiting for large deliveries such as barrels of sugar. They knew from experience that these were too bulky to go through the small entrance, and that Mr Harrod would scoop the cargo into a bucket and disappear for a few seconds while he discharged it inside. During those precious moments, the children would plunge their hands into the barrel, and by the time Harrod returned they were hurrying away with their loot spilling out between their fingers.

There was an unavoidable hurly-burly as goods came and went through the front doors of the shop, the only possible route. Charles Taylor, who joined the despatch team in 1881, found it worth hiring an extra truck at twopence per hour to help cope with the delivery load, and funded the equipment out of customers' tips.

## THE STRANGER ON THE BUS

Surprisingly for such a disciplined man, Harrod occasionally forgot to take any coins with him, and one day in 1882 he found himself stranded on a bus with no money. In acute embarrassment, he asked the man sitting next to him to loan him the amount of the fare, handing over his business card as a guarantee. The stranger was Edgar Cohen, a sponge importer, who readily

Charles Digby Harrod would have been travelling on an omnibus similar
to this one when he realised he had forgotten to bring any money with him and
would have to ask his neighbour to loan him the fare. This meeting with Edgar Cohen
became one of the legends in the store's history.

obliged with a half sovereign. The two men chatted about business for the
rest of the journey, and the next day Harrod sent a messenger with the cash.
As a result of this chance meeting, Cohen advised Harrod a number of
times over the next few years, and indeed later joined the board of Harrods.

## THE GREAT FIRE

The Christmas of 1883 promised to be the best yet for the store. Harrod had
stepped up his advertising to publicise the wide range of merchandise on
offer, and the premises were bursting with special goods on the night of 6
December. Kibble and Gearing, the despatch manager, were the last out of
the store at 11pm. Within minutes the building was on fire. Caused perhaps
by a gas lamp, or a stray flame from a builder's candle, the blaze spread
rapidly through the dry goods and their wrappings. Soon the Brompton
Road was a scene of dramatic and intense activity lit up by the flames as fire
engines from nine stations struggled with the blaze. There were 250 police
constables on hand to help and control the crowd, but they could not stop

the virtual destruction of the Harrods building. The *Chelsea Herald* of 8 December 1883 carried a graphic account of the incident:

It is particularly unfortunate that, just at the moment when these gigantic stores had been literally stocked to overflowing with Xmas goods – costaques and cards and more elaborate presents, to say nothing of the hogsheads and boxes of comestibles – that an outbreak of fire should have occurred. . . . From the raised pavement on the western side of Brompton Road a considerable crowd watched a scene of a splendidly terrible character. Only the skeleton of the three large shops and the stores at the back remained: but the fire raged in a seething mass shooting high up in the air from the inner portion, whilst the flames clung tenaciously to the window frames, mouldings, and other wood work, thus outlining the structure as if by an intentional illumination. The steam fire engine and hose from the hydrants were pouring tons of water upon the burning mass; but for a time with no apparent effect in even checking the conflagration. . . . Shortly before 2am there was a terrific rush of flame from the rear of the stores, caused apparently by the ignition of a quantity of spirits or other inflammables. The fearful heat thrown out by this caused a general stampede of all who were near the fire, which at that moment seemed to threaten with destruction the whole of the range of private dwellings.

Cynics among the crowd joked that this was another 'Whiteley's fire', as that department store was notorious for its flammability, to the annoyance of the insurance companies, who eventually refused cover on the building.

An aid was sent hurtling off in a hansom cab through the freezing streets to inform the boss. Harrod arrived in the middle of the night to see the ashes of his business drift through the air. Gearing, whose desk was next to Harrod's own, waded into the icy water next morning, retrieving the bank book. As a result he was taken ill and Harrod sent him three bottles of brandy a week until he recovered. The book he had rescued showed that Harrod had no debtors or creditors: the cash-only principle had paid off.

### CARRYING ON THROUGH ADVERSITY

The morning after the fire Harrod was installed at a table in a local public house issuing orders to his staff. Shortly after, customers received a letter, dated 7 December 1883, saying: 'I greatly regret to inform you that, in consequence of the above premises being burnt down, your order will be delayed in the execution a day or two. I hope, in the course of next Tuesday or Wednesday next, to be able to forward it. In the meantime may I ask for your kind indulgence.' His wife sent a message to Edgar Cohen asking for his help. Cohen found temporary premises for Harrods, renting nearby Humphrey's Hall, which had recently closed after housing a Japanese exhibition. Within three days the iron-framed building looked like a market. Thus Harrods was able to continue trading while the burnt-out store was being rebuilt over the next nine months.

Disastrous as the fire must have seemed at the time, it was the making of Harrods. In the first place, it allowed Harrod to create a new, purpose-built store which was far superior to the old, rambling shop. In the second place, extensive sympathetic coverage in the newspapers provided massive publicity for the store and ensured that no one in London could be ignorant of its existence and range of goods, or dismiss the fire as 'another Whiteley's'. Harrod therefore had an excellent reputation and considerable public sympathy on his side. When the new Harrod's Stores opened with 200 staff in September 1884, the firm's turnover doubled to £2,000 per week. (A description of the premises can be found on pages 47–49, and a contemporary account of the store appears on pages 111–115.)

## CASH DESKS AND ACCOUNT CUSTOMERS

William Kibble was in charge of the ground floor, and William Smart the sales areas above it. With Charles Harrod they handled all buying duties, including the new own-brand range, decked out in patriotic red, white and blue. Despite the tremendous workload resulting from this alone, they found time to introduce two major changes at the store. First, Harrod decided that it was pointless having messenger boys cluttering up the shop sprinting between counters with customers' change. He therefore set up cash desks at stations throughout the store, installing 'pay at the desk' signs on the counters to introduce the innovation to his customers. The importance of this move towards greater efficiency, which required the customer to do some of the work the shop previously covered, should not be underestimated.

Kibble and Smart seem to have been reluctant to make the change, but perhaps they compromised on it because of the second major innovation, which they had themselves introduced. This was to allow certain vetted customers to have an account, which meant persuading Harrod to break his 'no credit rule'. It is said that Oscar Wilde, Lillie Langtry and Ellen Terry were among those early honoured customers. Today there are 200,000 account customers.

Charles Henry Harrod, who had taken over the failing grocer's shop many years before, died in 1885. His mourning son Charles Digby, now 44, continued to put in gruelling, long days at the shop. (All staff worked a seventy-five hour week including meal breaks, which were taken at the counter.) Harrod's own health was not good, however, and he fainted in his office several times.

Despite this, Harrod retained a staunch grip on the business. We can picture him in 1887 on the sales floors, which were jammed with special novelty items celebrating Queen Victoria's golden jubilee. Twirling his keys, and issuing orders (ending with the familiar cry 'No humbugging') to his 200 staff, he was an all-pervasive influence on the store.

## FORMATION OF THE LIMITED COMPANY

A weary Charles Digby Harrod finally retired in 1889. Edgar Cohen – the stranger on the bus – advised him on the sale of the business, for Harrods was to be transformed into a limited liability company. A board of directors was formed, headed by London businessman Alfred Newton. Cohen advised Harrod to take payment in the form of the £1 founder's shares. Ever the man for cash, Harrod insisted on being bought out in bank notes instead, and eventually settled for £120,000, retiring to Somerset, and then to Sussex. He was later to buy some of those £1 shares at their new market value: £400.

The prospectus for the new company, Harrods Stores Limited, commented, 'The Stores are admirably situated, having an extensive frontage to a most important thoroughfare, and adjacent to perhaps the largest residential neighbourhood of London. ... the Directors consider that an annual profit of £20,000 may soon be anticipated.'

William Smart took over as general manager, and any chagrin Kibble felt at being overlooked for promotion must have turned to

182 REGENT ST. W.

Said to be among the first customers honoured with a Harrods account were (left to right) Oscar Wilde, Lillie Langtry and Ellen Terry.

deep concern as the shop's fortunes began to slide. Smart introduced a couple of new departments, but sloppiness and inefficiency crept into the everyday running of the store. The directors could see trouble in the balance sheets, but none had the retailing expertise to correct the slide. They appealed to Charles Digby Harrod, using Cohen as an intermediary. Cohen succeeded in persuading the founder's son that despite the fact that he had no shares in the company, the public would identify him with its failure, bringing shame on the family name.

Harrod returned and was shocked by the plummeting standards he discovered. He did what he could to put order into the shop's affairs, and began to search for a more competent replacement. The man he chose, and who was to be the architect of the store's rise to the status of a national institution, was Richard Burbidge.

## THE MAN FROM WHITELEY'S

Born in 1847, Richard Burbidge was the fourth of nine sons of Mr and Mrs George Bishop Burbidge. His father died when Richard was young, and in 1861 – the year Charles Digby Harrod took over the Knightsbridge store – Mrs Burbidge paid a London shopkeeper 100 guineas to take her son on and teach him the retail wine and provisions trade. He was a quick learner, for within a few years he began running a shop and speculating a little on the property market. He eventually ended up working at Whiteley's in Bayswater, then the largest store in London, and he was in charge for about eight years before taking a job running a new enterprise in Kensington.

The lucrative offer of £1,500 a year from Harrods came soon after his move, and Burbidge prevaricated, accepting it and then changing his mind. He was threatened with a court injunction by the shrewd Harrods chairman Alfred Newton before he finally joined the company in 1891! Some of the staff were equally wary of their new general manager, for Burbidge was known as a Whiteley's man. That shop had a reputation as a poor employer and was the only store in London that did not concern itself with references before taking on staff.

The Harrods staff were uneasy about Burbidge's commitment to his new firm. They saw him as a wandering spirit who had worked for a number of concerns in his career, and wondered how long he would stay. In fact, he worked for Harrods until his death, and two more generations of Burbidges were to become managing directors of the firm. Ironically, the Burbidge dynasty had a much greater and longer interest in Harrods than the founding family, and it was Burbidge who transformed the store into a national institution.

Richard Burbidge was a man of contrasts. He could be kindly and easygoing, but he had a ruthless streak. Hard-headed and soft-hearted, he possessed a very sharp mind and boundless energy, with a great enthusiasm for pursuing opportunities. He was rigidly self-disciplined, a non-drinker and a non-smoker. Fond of horses, Burbidge knew the danger of over-driving them, and he applied this knowledge to people. One of the first things he did was to reduce the store's opening hours by an hour a day, to close at 7pm every night except Fridays (still 8pm) and Saturdays (back an hour to 9pm). At the same time he stopped the fines for lateness and introduced cost-price meals for the staff.

## BURBIDGE'S DREAM

With his knowledge of the property market, Richard Burbidge was familiar with the concept of raising new money and paying it off through the increased return it fostered. An experienced store man, he relentlessly pursued a vision to expand the shop over the whole of the island site of

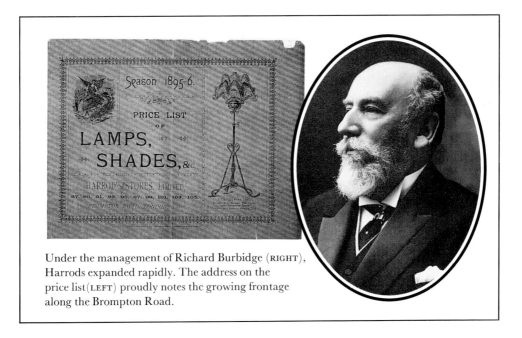

Under the management of Richard Burbidge (RIGHT), Harrods expanded rapidly. The address on the price list (LEFT) proudly notes the growing frontage along the Brompton Road.

which it then formed a part. Burbidge had visited some of the great American stores and had the idea of building a massive and diversified department store in London.

That autumn he asked the board for more capital, and the directors issued £100,000 of 5 per cent debentures (on a total capital of £140,000), putting the man who found the money, William Mendel, on the board. It was the first in a succession of share issues, some of them highly controversial, to raise capital and expand the business.

## A TYPICAL YEAR

Let us take one year, 1894, and see the progress the now firmly established Richard Burbidge was making. Its events show major changes to every aspect of the business, carried out at a breathtaking pace.

An advertisement from the mid 1890s, by which time Harrods could quote
an endorsement by a senior judge and was still reminding readers that there was
'no entrance fee or subscription required', unlike its rival Co-operative stores.

On 10 May a full-page advertisement (costing £200) in the *Daily
Telegraph*, headed by the slogan 'Harrods Serve the World' and the Latin
motto 'Omnia Omnibus Ubique' (Everything for Everybody Everywhere), quoted this testimonial: 'Lord Esher (Master of the Rolls) stated
from the Bench that Harrods Stores was one of the most interesting and
beautiful establishments in the whole of London.' Burbidge issued the
firm's largest catalogue yet, totalling 1,466 pages. The store supplied
countless picnic hampers containing 'all kinds of fancy dishes cooked and
garnished to suit the requirements of customers' for Henley Regatta Week.
A three-week cab strike which threatened trade led him to buy twenty
horses and cabs and start a livery stable offering customers transport.

During this year, as throughout his rule, Burbidge would meet the four
section managers at 10am and take a tour of the forty departments on the
premises (latest additions: furs, the bakery, hairdressing, photography and
the ground-floor restaurant). He was also working on deals to buy yet more
land around the store. Chairman Alfred Newton put Burbidge, who had
recently been made managing director, on to the board of DH Evans, the
Oxford Street store that was also in the group. To do this, Newton had to
over-ride the Harrods directors, who feared that their dynamic employee
would be sapped of his remarkable energy.

The staff enjoyed their first sports day on fourteen acres of land made available for their recreation next to the new depository at Barnes. Doubt-less much of the talk that day was of the new shop hours just brought in. Friday and Saturday closing time was now 7pm, and the 4pm shutdown on Thursday pioneered a move towards early closing one day a week. (The following year it became 2pm – and staff more used to the marathon hours of Mr Harrod's day could not believe their luck.) Amid all these develop-ments, profits were running at £30,000 a year.

## THE BENEVOLENT DICTATOR

Burbidge sustained this frenetic activity through the 1890s, putting in at least as many hours as Charles Digby Harrod had. But unlike his predecessor, Burbidge was not an exemplary Victorian: fired by his imagination, he was more of an opportunist. Although authoritarian, he pioneered a number of improvements for the staff, including a Provident Society and the establishment of the Harrodians Amateur Athletic Associ-ation. Consequently, the head of the firm was able to rule his staff through general high regard – although still a little tainted by fear. His desire to be liked was probably something of a handicap at times. After his son Woodman (who joined the firm in 1893) rose to a senior position, Richard Burbidge tended to pass to him the more unpleasant tasks such as sackings and placating angry customers.

Nor was Burbidge's judgement totally infallible. In 1897 he invested heavily in viewing seats in Haymarket, central London, for the huge procession marking Queen Victoria's diamond jubilee. The seats, which were to be sold at between 2 and 25 guineas each, did not sell. The loss of nearly £18,000 was the equivalent of almost a week's takings and a quarter of that year's profits. No doubt the board, of which he was now a part, registered their dismay. It would have been more than matched by his own consternation, for such setbacks slowed Harrods' progress in overtaking the rival Whiteley's store as the biggest in the city.

## EDWARDIAN ELEGANCE

With the end of the Victorian age (the indomitable queen died in 1901), Harrods entered the Edwardian era as the essence of elegance, style and dynamism. It was the largest department store in London and its dress salons were reputed to be the finest in Europe. Gathering employees at a dizzy pace – 3,000 in 1904, up to 4,000 by 1908 – the store passed the £2 million turnover mark in 1905, and began switching the accent from price to quality. Its reputation for top-class goods was strengthened by the introduction of London's first day-and-night telephone service. This was followed by free delivery anywhere in England and Wales, and of drapery to Scotland and Ireland, this latter service alone costing £10,000 per year. Advertisements boasted: 'Harrods... the Shrine of Fashion... The World's Greatest Emporium... one of the most commodious and elegant shops in the world'. Burbidge was shrewdly steering the store to a better class of customer than the mix of rich and poor that Charles Harrod had been happy to attract. The shift is exemplified by the introduction of a car hire facility in 1907.

The department store movement was far more advanced in the United States, and in 1908 an American, Gordon Selfridge, arrived in London announcing his intention to build a huge shop. Other retailers quaked as he selected a site in Oxford Street and proceeded to build a store with eight floors, three of them underground. It was the first purpose-built department store in the capital, and it made a massive impact on the retail scene. Selfridge's publicity was as brash and large-scale as the store, and it represented a very real threat to the old guard, led by Harrods and Whiteley's. They responded aggressively – Harrods' profits were considerably lower for the year as a result of its extensive counter-attack.

### DIAMOND JUBILEE CELEBRATIONS

How fortuitous it was that Harrods discovered that the very week Selfridges planned to open, in March 1909, coincided with its own sixtieth anniversary, to be celebrated with a 'Commemoration Week' to mark the diamond jubilee. Events included concerts performed in the store by the London Symphony Orchestra, described as 'a series of high class vocal and instrumental entertainments, which probably are entitled to rank as an unprecedented feature in the history of London retail business enterprise' by the trade paper *Draper's Record*. The journal had been recounting each stage of the contest with mounting excitement under headlines such as 'Battle of the Giants'. 'In addition,' continued the paper, 'the whole of the store will be converted into a huge bower of national flowers and in these beautiful surroundings the management will introduce its patrons to the first show of spring fashion novelties.' Staff were not forgotten, receiving an extra week's wages in recognition of their loyalty; the newcomer had tried to attract staff by boasting that it paid the best rates in town.

Even the *Draper's Record* felt Harrods had gone too far at one point, sternly intoning on 6 March 1909:

> The announcement made by Messrs Harrods this week must be
> regarded as a proposition of an entirely different order. Mr Haldane,
> Secretary of State for War, is to be the 'star' on the opening day of the
> Brompton Road store's 'Commemoration Week', and he will give an
> address on the Territorial Army... We think the trade generally were
> prepared to look with indulgent eye on Messrs Harrods's lapse from the
> recognised path of British retail trading, since the circumstances are
> exceptional. But this week's addition to the programme is, we repeat, a
> totally different matter. .... To enlist the services of a Cabinet Minister
> in this way has certainly never been attempted in commercial annals.

Let us make it clear that in what we have written we are not in any way hostile to the up-to-date firm that has added to its reputation for astuteness by its latest coup. On the contrary, some admiration must be felt for the enterprising methods by which the great Brompton Road store has been built up.

Clearly the journal felt that Harrods had gone too far in using a representative of the British establishment to help in its fight against the American pretender to its crown.

Further evidence that Harrods was prepared for a brawl rather than a little genteel sparring comes from the fact that this seems to have been the moment when it switched its house colours to green and gold. Could the move have been designed to limit the impact of the appearance of the fleet of Selfridge's vans on London roads, decked out in . . . green and gold?

Whatever the flag of convenience these events were sailing under, the celebrations emphasised how far the shop had come – not just in six decades, but in the eighteen years that Richard Burbidge had been captaining the ship. He turned a busy but not truly exceptional shop into the most fashionable, largest, best store in London, which a member of the government was prepared openly to support.

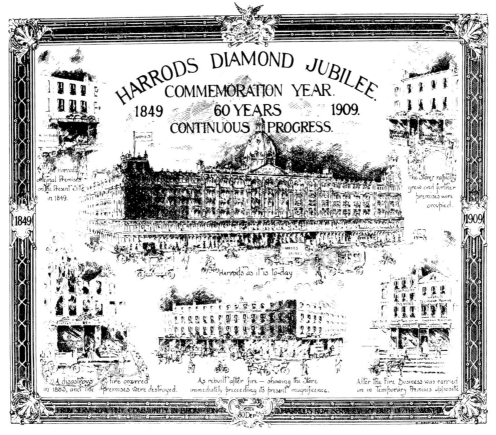

An illustration published in 1909 commemorating landmarks in Harrods' history.

Expansion and refurbishment have dominated the history of the Harrods
store, with the atmosphere of opulence and elegance carefully
preserved. This is the Fine Jewellery Room in 1990.

# CHAPTER THREE

## THE PREMISES

—— *Harrods* ——

# "An atmosphere of luxury and pleasure"

The special ambience that characterises Harrods can be partly attributed to its palatial premises. The elegance and splendour of the Edwardian era are still much in evidence today – largely as a result of major programmes of refurbishment through the years.

In its lifetime the Harrods building must have provided more work for refurbishment specialists than any other structure in London. Its story is one of extension, rebuilding and redesign in a cycle that seems destined never to end. The ongoing saga of construction work at Harrods stems from the fact that the building was not designed overall as a store at all (at one stage there was more space for private accommodation than retailing). It forms a complex three-dimensional jigsaw of bricks and mortar which can be relied upon to disorientate the most experienced surveyor.

### THE NEW STORE AFTER THE FIRE

In 1884 the new Harrod's Stores, built on the Brompton Road site where its predecessor had burnt down the year before, covered five floors and had a frontage on the Brompton Road of 55 metres/180 feet and a depth of 61 metres/200 feet. There were two storeys of sales areas, while the basement was used for storage. A circular counter in the middle of the shop was surrounded by well-stocked food departments. The focal point of the store was its grand central staircase, which was wide enough for three ladies in their full dresses to ascend side by side. It led to a floor stocked with hardwares of all kinds.

The shop was part of a large block split by a narrow road which was eventually built over in 1902–3. The block was occupied by other stores,

TOP: Harrods c. 1891, about two years after it became a limited company.
ABOVE: The store in 1892. Note that the Brompton Road frontage was still only one storey high.
The Buttercup public house is on the right.

[48]

By 1901, halfway through Richard Burbidge's
twenty-year expansion programme, Harrods was
beginning to dominate the Brompton Road.

three pubs (which were open all hours of the day and night) and a small
school. At its rear were some appalling slums, and many houses in this poor
district could be rented for as little as 9/6d per week.

Despite the impressive size of these premises for the time, it seems that
Charles Digby Harrod had underestimated the space he required for his
booming business. Within two years of the opening of the new store,
another extension took place, adding 24 metres/80 feet to the length of the
ground floor to make room for new departments.

## A VISION OF EXPANSION

When Richard Burbidge took over the running of Harrods in 1891, it was
his vision of expansion that led to the store covering the whole island site it
occupies today. It took him twenty years to achieve his dream, and
sometimes it must have seemed as if he would never make it.

Rapid progress was made in the first four months of 1893 with the
acquisition of 91–99 Brompton Road. Over the next two decades Burbidge
oversaw a long process of lease acquisition and rebuilding in an anti-
clockwise direction around the block he aimed to take over entirely. He
financed the buying and building with a series of share issues which aroused
some controversy in the financial press, but Burbidge had dabbled in
property for years and he knew what he was doing. He was acquiring

TOP AND ABOVE: The Brompton Road frontage, c. 1904, when work on the
imposing terracotta facade was nearing completion.

properties and harvesting extra space from them, so that they could be filled with new ranges of goods; it was a remarkably bold and clear-sighted programme. In retrospect it is easy to gain the impression of steady and planned progress. The reality was a lot less clearcut, with each stage forming a complex project in its own right.

For example, it took Burbidge several years to persuade his neighbour Mrs DeCoster to sell up her drapery shop. His eventual success not only brought him more space but also freed him from an old agreement not to sell rival drapery goods. The next year he reported a significant rise in turnover, partly attributed to sales of drapery goods.

While Burbidge was haggling with the extremely stubborn Mrs DeCoster, he was also buying up slum land (at 1/9d per square foot) behind the store, and leasing what he could not purchase outright. Again the benefits were twofold: he gained more space, and by ridding his neigh-bourhood of slums he raised the tone of the whole of Knightsbridge.

## RAPID BUT CONTROLLED PROGRESS

Burbidge would roam the building sites checking on progress when a project was under way. His grandchild 'Mr Richard' later commented that 'my love of this business was instilled into me ever since I was a boy of five and my grandfather used to take me over the scaffolding at the back of Hans Road'. By 1896, the *Daily Telegraph* was able to report in some detail on the expansion taking place:

Harrod's Stores is a firm which has by dint of capable and judicious management extended and magnified itself in a wonderful manner within comparatively few years. In fact, so great has the business become of late that to fully cope with the needs and demands of the host of patrons, it has been found necessary to add an extensive set of new buildings to the old. To the ordinary outsider the exterior appearance of the Brompton emporium does not lead him to expect the vastness of the present interior. The new adjuncts, which are built on freehold ground purchased at a cost of £80,000, are at once attractive, roomy and in every way a fine addition to the old. The ground floor of the new buildings, which cover an area of 26,000 square feet, with a frontage of 400 feet, also includes extensions for jewellery, music, pictures, trunks, saddlery, and all 'sporting' requisites. The handsome dining rooms have been set up in the François Premier style. Portraits of contemporaries of that monarch ornament the walls, the lower part of which are panelled, and a general air of luxury pervades the whole place. An entirely new departure is the installation of a safe deposit on the lines. . . of the National Safe Company. There is a large number of small safes for rental, and every precaution is naturally taken to ensure the safe guardance of the contents.

At this time the Basil Street and Hans Crescent sides of the site (on the southern and eastern boundaries respectively) were five storeys high. The upper three floors were devoted to meeting demand for the latest property fad: apartments. Richard Burbidge was shrewd enough to ensure that the flats met the requirements of the top end of the market. Featuring sizeable and well decorated rooms, they were planned around light wells which allowed sunlight into skylights above the showrooms – one is still readily identifiable today in the Meat Hall. The flats provided Harrods with valuable income for many years. (This arrangement was common in the late nineteenth century – most of Regent Street began in the same way.)

The Brompton Road side of the store, with its major frontage, was much as it had been on the original shop nearly half a century before, with The Buttercup public house on the corner. This pub was a sizeable thorn in Burbidge's side, for it occupied a valuable corner site and lowered the tone of the area. Ironically, the pub thrived partly because it was frequented by so many Harrods staff, who enjoyed being able to relax after their long hours of toil within a few paces of their workplace. The landlord refused to sell his lucrative lease, but Burbidge, enterprising as ever, came up with an ingenious proposition: the pub would vacate the premises and the landlord would pay Harrods £15,000 in return for the store finding him a comparable site elsewhere. Perhaps out of sheer surprise at the audacity of being asked to pay Harrods for the privilege of moving, the man behind the pumps agreed, and Burbidge closed the deal at 10.30 one night. With his new strongroom locked up for the night, he strolled contentedly back to his flat above the store with the cash – which was equivalent to a quarter of the year's profits. Burbidge never managed to find his former neighbour a better site, and eventually Harrods had to buy off the landlord with £25,000, but Burbidge had got what he wanted.

In the same year, 1897, Burbidge also secured the leases of 111–115 Brompton Road, plus the school site at the rear. These leases had five years to run, so he knew that in 1902 he would be able to expand the store's frontage, in effect doubling it, and gain access at the back of the building.

At this time he was also refitting the old soap works near the Thames at Barnes which he had bought in 1894 for £16,200. This was to become the Barnes depository, at one time one of the largest warehouses in Europe, with space for 6,000 pantechnicon loads. It became something of a landmark during the Oxford vs Cambridge Boat Race, when thousands of radio listeners and later television viewers were thrown into confusion by the commentator explaining 'and now they are just going past Harrods'.

## LONDON'S FIRST 'MOVING STAIRCASE'

Richard Burbidge wanted more lateral space for the store because he did not believe customers were prepared to trek up many flights of stairs to shop; and despite his frequent visits to American stores, he loathed lifts. His obstinacy reaped huge benefits in publicity when he installed London's first escalator, in 1898. More like a conveyor belt with handrails than a modern escalator, the moving staircase ran 12 metres/40 feet up a gradual slope from the ground to the first floor. Burbidge recorded in his diary that it

Customers hurry to ride the famous
moving staircase – London's first
escalator – to the next floor.

could carry 4,000 people per hour. But apart from its transportation benefits, the device inspired wide publicity. The *Daily Chronicle* waxed poetic about travellers being 'wafted by imperceptible motion' and *the Sketch* said, 'By a delightful movement, which is both exhilarating and fascinating, you are carried from floor to floor without the least effort, and without any of those unpleasant thrills which lifts always succeed in giving

LEFT: This closing-down sale leaflet marked Burbidge's success in buying out his neighbour's drapery store. CENTRE: Harrods' frontage in 1902.
RIGHT: The frontage in 1904, revealing the dramatic expansion of the store at this time – and the increasing traffic on the Brompton Road.

nervous persons.' Those of a nervous disposition were catered for: an attendant on the first floor comforted any customers flustered by the experience with a choice of free doses of sal volatile (smelling salts) or cognac. The contraption was replaced by lifts in 1909.

In 1901 an advertisement in the *Daily Mail* announced a rebuilding sale, explaining with a hint of pride, 'To cope with the continually increasing volume of business the directors have decided to at once rebuild and enlarge the shops ranging from 87 to 99 Brompton Road and 1 to 7 Hans Crescent which will entail the temporary removal of the whole Drapery Section to 107 to 109 Brompton Road, premises recently acquired by the company.' By this time the store was dominating a much broader Brompton Road, as the increased traffic from horse carriages and even the odd daring soul in a motor vehicle had led to the street being widened.

## THE DOULTON CONNECTION

With the Brompton Road frontage acquired, a new and elaborate facade was erected, with a central dome and carved pediments. It was designed by architect CW Stephens, whose portfolio included work for Claridges and also for Harvey Nichols, the neighbouring store. The imposing terracotta facade, supplied by Doulton, was built in five sections between 1901 and

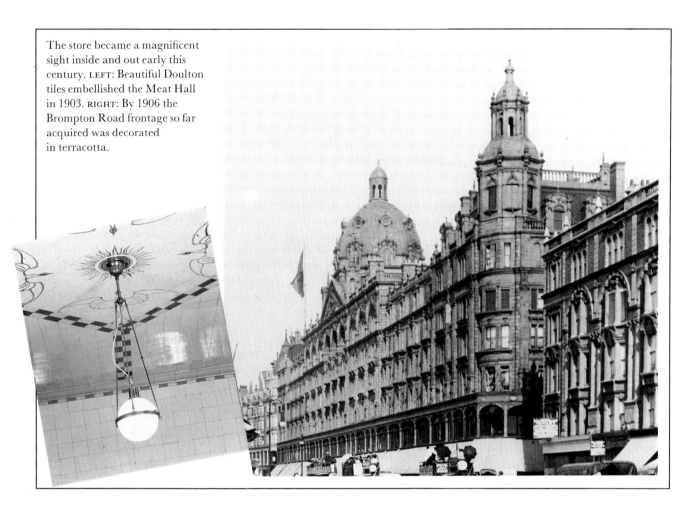

The store became a magnificent sight inside and out early this century. LEFT: Beautiful Doulton tiles embellished the Meat Hall in 1903. RIGHT: By 1906 the Brompton Road frontage so far acquired was decorated in terracotta.

1905, and represented a major step towards gaining the full island site. The final block, measuring 24 metres/80 feet by 37 metres/120 feet, was demolished and rebuilt in six weeks – the frantic pace providing evidence of the pressure builders were under to minimise inconvenience to shoppers.

The changes to the premises were not merely external. In 1902–3 the Meat Hall was built on the site of the old school. It was decorated with Doulton tiles, designed by WJ Neatby, showing scenes from the hunt. These are regarded as such fine examples of Edwardian decor that they are now under a preservation order.

## SELF-SUFFICIENCY

The Meat Hall required cold storage, and in 1903 Harrods' engineers were busy behind the scenes setting up a huge support service, storage and workroom infrastructure. First, they bored three artesian wells, the deepest falling to 149 metres/489 feet below ground level. These wells, sunk into London chalk, supply excellent pure water for the store to this day. The water was also used for making ice. Huge blocks of it were placed at the bottom of the air shafts during the summer to create a supply of cool air around the store. (The air in Harrods is changed eight times an hour.) The store still produces for itself the water needed to make the two tons of ice

[55]

required daily to preserve foods, provide drinking water, operate toilets, etc – a total of more than 122 million litres/27 million gallons a year.

When they had put in the wells, the engineers were kept busy installing steam engines and coal-fired boilers to produce electricity for the store. From the introduction of these in 1908 until 1921, Harrods had no use for outside electrical supplies; it met all its needs itself. This self-sufficiency in water and electricity appealed to the shrewd Richard Burbidge, who preferred money to be spent for the benefit of the store, not outsiders. To this day, Harrods generates about 70 per cent of the electricity it consumes – which is in itself enough to supply a small town.

Despite his success on the Brompton Road, Burbidge was meeting with less satisfaction in obtaining the leases on the Hans Road frontage. These buildings were mainly houses, with occupants who had no reason to move from what was now one of the most fashionable parts of London.

## EDWARDIAN SPLENDOUR

In 1909 the Brompton Road frontage had been extended to 133 metres/435 feet, to which was added 111 metres/365 feet in Hans Crescent, 91 metres/300 feet in Basil Street, and 113 metres/370 feet in Hans Road. The Brompton Road frontage was decked out in terracotta on a granite base with fittings of gun metal and mahogany. This exterior design with embellishments picked out in bright colours was very much the fashion, as colour had become a feature of street architecture.

The Harrods Royal Exchange in 1909. Likened to a marble palace, it was famous for its marble walls, fine statuary and furniture of mahogany and leather.

An artist's impression of the store exterior in Edwardian times, following the completion of the terracotta facade by Doulton.

Inside the store, each department was decorated in a different but equally grand style, the whole being connected by archways. The huge ground floor Royal Exchange was walled in marble and furnished with Spanish mahogany upholstered in green Moroccan leather. The Millinery department featured elaborately modelled and painted ceilings over richly carved fittings in ancona walnut. The store's publicity advised customers in the Ladies' Hairdressing courts to study the polished satinwood woodwork carving 'in the Egyptian style with introductions of superb Marqueterie panelling'. The publicity material also waxed lyrical about the Ladies' Club:

> The larger of the rooms is furnished in Adam style in figured satinwood. The chairs are upholstered in green corded silk, tastefully decorated with appliqué embroidery. Indian carpets are laid over the oak parquet floor. The retiring room is nicely fitted out, the effect in marble being admirable. The windows are stained cathedral glass, while the walls are covered throughout with panelled Brecchi Sanguine, Pavannazi, levantine marble and onyx panels, the whole rendering a unique effect.

It makes the Gentlemen's Club (early Georgian style in carved and moulded mahogany) sound tame by comparison. Most spectacular of all was the roof over the Food Halls: a 9 metre/30 foot high ornamental glass dome, set off below by beautifully coloured tiles.

By 1910 Knightsbridge was welcoming numerous day-visitors on their way to the enlarged Victoria and Albert Museum nearby. Many were able to travel on the newly opened Piccadilly underground line. The store itself, unusually opulent for a shop, was one of the major attractions of the area. Strolling around all its departments took more than two hours.

## THE TOWER THAT NEVER WAS

Under Richard Burbidge's relentless guidance, more premises in Hans Road were acquired in 1911, and at last Harrods owned the whole 18,000 square metre/4.5 acre island site of which it had once been a minor element. Rather than offering a chance for a break from property leases and architects' plans, the achievement hurled Burbidge into a new bout of activity. He wanted to erect a 61 metre/200 foot tower on the store to commemorate the coronation of George V, but the plan was abandoned when

A 1911 illustration showing the store complete with the
Coronation Tower that was never built.

residents objected. A stone marking the laying of its foundation, dated 13 September 1911, rests in Hans Road as permanent evidence of the attempt. What is more, some Harrods brochures published in that year included an illustration of the store with the tower already in place!

But this was a mere diversion for the managing director. He still needed more space, and in 1912 a site across the road in Trevor Square was purchased for storage, despatch, bakeries and factory use.

## BEWILDERING LABYRINTH

The purchase set a new challenge for the engineers. They had already constructed a network of white-tiled tunnels under the store. These were given suburban names such as Frosty Way (towards the ice rooms) and Wine Cellar Close. Now a new tunnel had to be sunk under the Brompton Road to provide an underground link with the Trevor Square building.

The warren of subways has changed little over the years, forming a maze that would cause the most accomplished orienteer to blanch. As staff hurried through the tunnels, they had to dodge innumerable trolleys and electric trucks clattering along. The subways were not areas of quiet contemplation: they echoed with rumbling wheels, shouted instructions and muttered complaints, and a notice was issued forbidding whistling in the tunnels because it was 'unbusinesslike'.

Beautiful and elaborate tilework in the Food Halls dates from early this century. This example is from the Floral Hall and was produced in 1925.

### THE POST-WAR PREMISES

After World War I, Sir Woodman Burbidge, who had succeeded his father as managing director in 1917 and who became chairman in 1921, was not convinced that the building would be big enough to handle the ambitious plans he had for it. For several years he nursed a plan to transfer Harrods to a completely new shop on the Trevor Square site. It was only the financial pressures of the Depression years in the 1920s that foiled this attempt to move the store from the land it had always occupied. He shifted his target and opted for vertical, rather than lateral expansion, converting flats on the level immediately above the store into sales areas. The last of the second-floor flat dwellers moved out in 1924, and four years later he had to move his own residence to the fourth floor to avoid its becoming a showroom! The lofty decorative ceilings of the apartments were perfectly compatible with the lavish decor on the other floors.

TOP: By 1924 the store exterior had long been completed, and it remains unchanged today.
ABOVE LEFT: The silver miniature of the store which was won as a result of a bet with Selfridges over who would achieve the highest turnover. It shows the store as it looked in the late 1920s.
ABOVE RIGHT: This beautifully finished skylight was installed above the Georgian Restaurant in 1929 and features three bays of intricate wrought iron scrollwork and floral decoration.

The Children's department in 1919 was as airy and spacious as the other
clothing departments. Harrods has a long tradition of meeting the needs of
its customers' children, who in turn become regulars themselves.

The store as it looked at this point is preserved in the form of a silver
reproduction – the result of a bet between Sir Woodman and Gordon
Selfridge of the rival department store in Oxford Street. In 1917 the
American had wagered that he would overtake Harrods in turnover within
six years of the declaration of peace after World War I. Ten years on, Sir
Woodman reminded his competitor that no such feat had been achieved,
and asked that instead of the previously agreed prize of a silver miniature of
the loser's store, he should receive a model of his own establishment. The
model of the Harrods store cost £400 – a considerable sum today, and a
small fortune at the time.

## SIGNS OF THE TIMES

Unhindered by his late father's prejudice against lifts, Sir Woodman
installed a battery of eight new ones serving all floors, taking the total
number of passenger lifts at the store to more than thirty. Another sign of

The Banking Hall in the 1940s, following major rebuilding work in
the mid-1930s. The floor was insulated to preserve the dignified hush.

the times was the addition of parking space for 100 cars: the days of the
carriage trade were over. So, however, were the times of automatic growth,
and in 1928 refurbishment work was postponed due to the depressed
economic conditions. When it resumed a year later the engineers faced a
new challenge with the collapse of an iron stanchion in the southwest
corner of the store. Hydraulic jacks slowly eased up the surrounding area to
make room for extra foundations to be put in.

More of the difficulties this colossal building poses to the construction
industry – and the scale of activity involved in altering it – were revealed
during additional rebuilding in February 1934. The sheer thickness of the
foundations caused a long hold-up in the work, and rebuilding was not in
full swing until August. Then in nine weeks 50,000 tons of building were
pulled down and carted away, and 80,000 tons of building materials
and fittings were brought in. Twenty vehicles an hour unloaded it, day
and night, for sixty-three days. With 5.6 km/3.5 miles of steel girder
weighing 1,000 tons successfully installed, the result could be seen. The new
Banking Hall, still walled with marble, stretched 90 metres/100 yards
across the ground floor. Its floor was now insulated with 1,000 rubber tiles
to keep the noise of a hundred hurrying customers to a dignified hush.

## A MAJOR ATTRACTION

Combining Edwardian splendour with some modern touches, the Harrods
building itself became a major attraction. According to an advertisement of

1932, 'The main building, together with Harrods' various factories, refrigerators, and warehouses, with which it is connected by a marvellous network of tiled subways, occupies a greater area than St Pauls Cathedral, The Bank of England, and the Tower of London combined.' The advertisement adds that this vast edifice is 'stocked with an unexampled wealth of merchandise ranging from the simplest daily need to the rarest, most sumptuous and costliest products of the earth. Visitors from overseas tell us that it is the most beautiful store in the world.'

At about this time it was recorded that a customer lift was leaving the ground floor every seven seconds, and that the equipment averaged 30,000 passenger trips a week. Even this was not enough for Sir Woodman, who had new escalators installed on the eastern side of the store in a major project in 1939. Like other rebuilding projects, the work had to be accomplished without reducing the number of departments and at minimum inconvenience to customers. Ongoing work therefore had to be hidden behind boards while allowing full access to all parts of the shop, and as much work as possible had to be scheduled outside trading hours. Added to these restrictions was the difficulty of coping with an ageing structure.

## THE HARRODS TUBE SYSTEM

Some fascinating work was also going on behind the scenes at the store in the 1930s. A message-carrying pneumatic tube system had been in use since Edwardian times, but the 1935 Sale saw the introduction of a system that carried cash as well. It was claimed to be the largest such system in the British Empire: 63 km/39 miles of twisting pipes. Customers' money was placed in a tube and swept at 27 km/17 miles an hour down to the basement. Cashiers placed the right change in the tube, adjusted the

The cash tube system in full swing around 1950. Introduced in 1935, the capsules sped from the counters down to this basement room, where they were returned with the correct change for the transaction.

Early in the century Harrods invested in elegant fittings. LEFT: An art nouveau influence can be seen in this entrance dating from around 1904 (photographed in the 1920s). TOP: The stylised bronzework of this bannister rail was the vogue in 1936.
ABOVE: Some beautiful wrought-iron scrollwork from 1903.

destination number, and sent it back. The longest journey was 400 metres/ one-quarter mile, and took 54 seconds. Engineers wearily, and repeatedly, explained to staff the importance of putting the tubes in the right way round, as otherwise the system became spectacularly clogged up. Seen as something of a technological miracle at the time, the system was still in use for carrying messages until the 1980s.

In fact very little of the building changed at all in the four decades from the early 1930s to the beginning of the 1970s. War damage was slight and, apart from the inevitable changes in department functions and locations and the addition of lifts, Harrods stayed much as it was during this period. 'Modernisation' of the Food Halls entailed covering some of its beautiful ceramic tiles, but these were rediscovered and returned to public view in the 1970s. The board directed more attention to acquiring other stores to build up the Harrods Group, with a special push after World War II to buy up blitzed department stores such as John Walsh in Sheffield. A noteworthy but largely unseen improvement came in 1961 when major work in straightening the subway tunnels was undertaken. This involved moving columns each supporting 300 tons of the building, so that more than one trolley could pass at a time.

## MODERN INNOVATIONS

It took the arrival of the far-sighted managing director Robert Midgley, in 1971, to force through major changes in the store's traditional layout and systems. The huge ground floor Banking Hall, by now something of an anachronism, was transformed into an elegant Perfumes Hall, furnished in red velvet and marble. The Food Halls were refurbished, many departments refitted, and the restaurants redesigned. A few years later the fourth floor management offices and directors' suites were ripped out to make space for the new sports department Olympic Way.

## THE HARRODS MAJOR PROJECT

In 1979 Harrods' chief engineer came up with some proposals for the biggest structural alteration for forty years, the installation of escalators on the northwest side of the store, off Hans Road. Preparing for the installation took eighteen months, as the builders struggled to create a big-enough hole for ten flights of escalators in a store already bursting at the seams. But it was worth the wait: one Sunday, all the escalators were installed between 6am and 9pm. The small team of workmen nervously watched each of the ten 9.5 ton flights sway in the wind from the crane, which positioned them to an accuracy of 2.5 cm/1 inch. Built in the grand Harrods style, the escalators were faced in Roman travertine marble and were set next to a waterfall, flanked by flowers, on the ground floor.

The work was just part of a major rebuild early in the 1980s. Known as the Harrods Major Project, it included the creation of 3,716 square metres/

40,000 square feet more selling space on the fourth floor, the launch of the kitchen goods Cook's Way department, the addition of two new Food Halls, as well as the installation of additional escalators, which have proved more popular with customers than the fifty lifts at the store.

One of the escalator flights being painstakingly winched
into place on the northwest side of the store.

## MAXIMISING ASSETS

The Food Halls gleamed anew in 1984 as the Fruit and Vegetable Halls were refurbished at a cost of £3.3 million. Once again customers could enjoy the original Royal Doulton tiles, which had been hidden behind panels for more than forty years. The tiles, depicting hyacinth-blue exotic birds and gilded urns laden with fruit, were complemented in 1987 by colourful swirling relief work of fruit and flowers on the ceilings, together with Louis Philippe-style chandeliers. The effect is spectacular.

The work has continued with a major move to transform the fifth floor, where many of the offices moved from lower floors had come to rest. These are now being banished for ever as Harrods begins to use the area as

sales space. The new Olympic Way complex is housed here, forcing yet more sections of the store administration out into Trevor Square. The basement, too, has been called in for duty as a salesroom. As the store was besieged with bargain hunters during the 1990 July Sale, 350 building workers were hammering and drilling away on this project beneath the feet of the oblivious shoppers.

## OPULENCE AND COMPUTER WIZARDRY

In 1987 Mohamed Al Fayed, owner of the store, announced a £200 million on-going refurbishment programme to recreate the opulent shopping environment of the store earlier in the century. The first stage of the programme was the unveiling of the new Leather Room, where green marble pillars and art deco bronze grills stand by counters dating back to the 1920s. Work on this and later phases has involved giving marble a specially cleaved finish so that it looks polished but is not slippery. Harrods

At night Harrods sparkles with the light of more than 11,000 bulbs.

is also installing lighting in the style of the 1920s and 1930s but with the energy-efficiency required of the 1990s.

One of the most memorable sights in London is the illuminated Harrods building at night. The building is lit up with 11,500 bulbs, which are gas-filled for extra sparkle, and replaced twice a year by electricians working on a 52 metre/170 foot mobile platform.

As more and more of the Harrods building has been devoted to sales space, increasing pressure has been put on the company's other premises. The Barnes depository, once the most modern warehouse of its kind, has been replaced by a new distribution centre at Osterley, west London. The £25 million centre, thought to be the most advanced in the world, comprises a massive warehouse with an 18 metre/59 foot-high racking system, storing four million items of stock which are stacked and retrieved by computerised trucks and cranes. It all seems a long way from the narrow alleyways of Victorian London!

Harrods decked out for the
Coronation of Queen Elizabeth II.

# CHAPTER FOUR

# THE PLACE TO BE SEEN

*Harrods*

# "The meeting place of Society"

Harrods has retained a reputation as the 'top people's store' for almost a century, maintaining its standing as part of society's elite through a succession of social changes. The key to this hold over a fickle market has been the store's preservation of its own extraordinary kudos. Harrods' great achievement has been to maintain its exclusivity while attracting and serving as many customers as possible.

## ROYAL PATRONAGE

Britain's Royal Family have for many years been regular visitors to the prestigious store conveniently situated just down the road from Buckingham Palace. Harrods is known as the 'Royals' Store', and has been delighted to welcome royalty from abroad for a long time, too. Indeed, the first royal warrant awarded to Harrods came in 1910 and allowed it to state that it was a furnisher and draper to the Queen of Norway (who was British – before her marriage she had been Princess Maud, daughter of Princess Alexandra and Edward VII). At this time Harrods was already receiving the regular custom of royal visitors from around the globe.

Mr John Hendrick Lovendahl, of the Silver and Jewellery department, welcomed all royal personages and was known as 'The Royal Shopwalker'. The list of those he greeted, reading like a *Who's Who* of international royalty, includes Queen Mary, Queen Alexandra (wife and then widow of Edward VII), the Queen and King of Norway, Prince Olaf of Norway, Princess Victoria, Princess Mary, the Queen of Spain, the King of Sweden, Princess Christian, Princess Henry of Battenberg, Princess Louise (Duchess of Argyll), Princess Patricia, King Mañuel, Queen Amelia, the Grand

Duchess Marie and the Grand Duke George of Russia, Prince George of Greece, the Grand Duke Ferdinand of Austria, the Queen of Roumania, the Duchess of Albany, and the Duke and Duchess of Connaught.

All these distinguished customers were met at the appointed hour and conducted round the store by the attentive Mr Lovendahl, who became well acquainted with several of his 'regulars' such as Queen Alexandra. Visits by such personages would have been well-known to the leading lights of society, and the royal patronage of the time did a great deal to foster the store's reputation as the place where the cream of society shopped. Harrods was even brought in as an interior decorator by Crown Prince Carol of Roumania to furnish Jarka House in Bucharest in 1921.

## VISITING HEADS OF STATE

Good service is part of the Harrodian ethos, and the store has always been prepared to go to particular lengths to accommodate the needs of prestigious customers, such as visiting heads of state. For example, when

LEFT: The Prince of Wales (later Edward VIII), with Sir Woodman Burbidge, at Harrods' 1932 Home Produce Exhibition. RIGHT: Queen Mary and Princess Mary visiting the store in 1919. On the left is Sir Woodman Burbidge.

the Emir of Katsina (Nigeria) stopped off at the store on his way to Mecca in 1921, no one batted an eyelid when he and his party declined the seats in Sir Woodman Burbidge's office and squatted on the floor in a semi-circle around his desk. When he explained that his two wives were forbidden from visiting the store, several assistants were despatched to their hotel to model the latest silks and satins. On a second visit, according to the *Harrodian*

*Gazette*, the staff newspaper, 'much time was occupied in discussing mouth washes. The Emir insisted that he must have a mouth wash that was non-alcoholic. When it was explained that this presented no difficulty, the Emir seemed much pleased.'

Rulers come and go, but a reputation has its own life. Nearly forty years later, on the eve of Nigerian independence, Harrods designed and manufactured a mace and 200 ceremonial staffs for the president of the House of Chiefs in Eastern Nigeria.

Harrods is well aware that the rulers of today can be the refugees of tomorrow, but however their status changes, customers can expect its best service. Thus the store was happy to accommodate the needs of one Serge Garkovenko, who wrote to the Safe Deposit manager from the Russian Consulate General in Shanghai, China, arranging for a friend to collect the contents of his vault: 'About 20 May 1919 I left in your department one large yellow trunk and one fibre brown valise, both full with my clothes and other things. I paid in advance for one year. During my escape from the Bolsheviks in April last I lost all my documents, papers and your receipt too. But if my memory is correct the pass word which is "Serge" will be sufficient to prove my identification.' At least he was alive. The last Tsar of Russia and his family had been killed in the Russian Revolution; only a few years before, two of his children had visited Harrods, where sailor suits were bought for them.

## QUEEN MARY'S LOYAL CUSTOM

Harrods is best known for meeting the needs of the British Royal Family, a reputation which originated with the loyal custom given by Queen Mary (consort of George V) throughout her life. Queen Mary's last visit to the store was in 1951.

Although some royal visits were private occasions, others attracted a great deal of attention. For example, when both Queen Mary and Princess Mary came to inspect the china and pottery exhibition on 30 April 1913, a large crowd gathered outside the store. Unfortunately, many waited outside the wrong entrance and were still there an hour after the visit had ended, having failed to catch so much as a glimpse of the royal party!

Harrods got rather more satisfaction from the event. The Queen said that she 'appreciated the commercial advantage likely to result from the exhibition of British goods of such beauty in the heart of a wealthy and cultured community like that served by Harrods'. In addition, Queen Mary granted Harrods a special warrant of appointment as drapers and furnishers to Her Majesty. (By 1919 Harrods held similar appointments for the royal families of Belgium and Italy, as well as being goldsmiths, silversmiths and silk mercers to Queen Alexandra.)

Such was the close relationship between Buckingham Palace and Harrods that the store was the automatic choice of supplier when extra

Princesses Elizabeth and Margaret leave Harrods with their mother, Queen
Elizabeth, after the royal Christmas shopping visit in 1938.

beds were required to accommodate guests at Buckingham Palace for the
coronation of George VI in 1937.

If Queen Mary's limousine was so much as a minute early at the store
she would instruct the chauffeur to tour the block once so that she arrived
exactly on time at Door 3 (her usual entrance point, which most of the
Royal Family continue to use).

## YOUNG ROYALS' VISITS

By 1939 Queen Mary was bringing her granddaughter Princess Elizabeth
along, and an account of their visit to the Pets Corner relates, 'The Queen
showed much interest in all things displayed, while Princess Elizabeth
selected collars and a bed for her own Corgi dog.'

When Princess Elizabeth married Prince Philip in 1946, Harrods
allowed one member of each department a day off to see the wedding.
Their son, Prince Charles, was taken to Harrods for his first-ever shopping
expedition, which was on the eve of his second birthday in 1951. The royal
toddler beamed with delight when he reached the Toy Fair and was so
eager to try out the roundabout that a great deal of tact was required to
persuade him to continue his tour. Staff report that when he chanced upon
a set of sleeping dolls he began looking among them for his baby sister
Anne. At the end of his tour, as the little Prince was escorted to the royal

car, he thanked his guide Mr Davidson and then asked enviously, 'Are you going back in there?'

### QUEEN ELIZABETH'S REGULAR VISITS

Queen Elizabeth's accession to the throne in 1952 did not stop her regular visits to the store, and a Harrods assistant wrote in December 1953:

> We members of the Harrodian family will have a very personal interest in the crowning of our young and radiant Queen, since many of us at Knightsbridge have been privileged to attend her on her many visits to the store as Princess and we all felt a thrill on her visiting us just before Christmas as Queen, for we realised that history was in the making: the British sovereign does not by custom shop personally.

The Royal Family's Christmas shopping trip had become an established ritual at the store by then, and Queen Elizabeth has remained a regular customer. In fact, the colour of her dark green Daimler, so often seen waiting outside the store, inspired Harrods chief cutter and designer Basil Rubython to make an unusual green dinner jacket, which won a trade prize in 1960.

Much of the British Royal Family shops at Harrods to this day. Toy section staff in particular have grown quite used to watching Princes William and Henry, sons of the Prince and Princess of Wales, trying out the latest games in their department.

### THE ROYAL WARRANTS

Today the store holds four royal warrants: suppliers of provisions and household goods to HM the Queen; suppliers of china, glass and fancy goods to HM Queen Elizabeth the Queen Mother; outfitters and saddlers to HRH the Prince of Wales; and outfitters to HRH the Duke of Edinburgh.

### A SOCIAL HISTORY

The history of Harrods tells the story of the society it serves, and tracing the development of the store provides some revealing insights into the changing world of the last 150 years. Harrods was fortunate to be situated in a

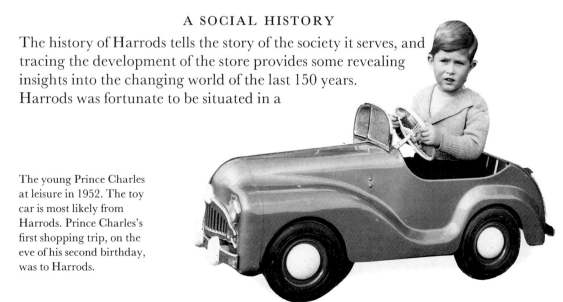

The young Prince Charles at leisure in 1952. The toy car is most likely from Harrods. Prince Charles's first shopping trip, on the eve of his second birthday, was to Harrods.

location which was adopted by the top echelons of society. Through the second half of the nineteenth century, London expanded as the nation prospered and the Empire grew, and there was a residential migration westwards. The population of the increasingly office-dominated City fell from 128,000 in 1851 to 75,000 twenty years later, at a time when the overall population of London was rising. (By the turn of the century, the London population had doubled from the 1851 figure of 2.25 million.)

The most fashionable place to live was along the Bayswater Road just north of Hyde Park. Kensington was also popular, and Knightsbridge, being nearer the centre of London, appealed to the moneyed merchants who travelled in to conduct their business. Although there were still slums in the area, London's west side was far more salubrious than the east, where Jack the Ripper stalked the murky alleyways, beginning his grisly series of murders in 1888.

The growth of a highly populated urban society led to a greater need for the upper classes to assert their status through possessions. Women began to wear more elaborate and colourful clothes (although silk dresses were frowned upon as implying easy virtue), and to change their outfits several times a day. Fashions in clothing began to come and go at a faster rate. All these developments increased the need for shopping trips. The invention of the sewing machine facilitated mass production of clothing. This meant that the upper classes, though they would have a tailor or dressmaker for some of their needs, were also able to purchase ready-to-wear garments. Other major status symbols included a capacious carriage manned by liveried servants; and pet dogs, a sign that the owner had sufficient money, space and leisure time to own the animal.

## THE CARRIAGE TRADE

High society was at its most active during the London 'Season'. Coinciding with the Parliamentary session from Easter to August, it brought the country gentry into town, accompanied by wives and daughters eager for the lively social life (and potential husbands) of London.

In the 1870s part of the routine during the Season was for gentlemen to parade of a morning in Hyde Park, where they would be joined by the ladies' carriages at noon. What could be more convenient than to take a short ride to that excellent Knightsbridge establishment, Harrod's Stores, for a little decorous shopping?

The shop permitted dogs to be chained to its railings (before eventually building its own kennels to accommodate customers' pets, a unique facility which survived until recently). As customers descended from their carriages, the store's accomplished shopwalkers would politely greet them and escort them to the desired department. Here they would be seated in comfortable chairs while assistants showed the latest stock.

These wealthy customers considered it demeaning to cart any but the

In Victorian and Edwardian times, high society took the air in London's
fashionable Hyde Park. This illustration from a Harrods promotional
booklet features Edwardian fashions which could be purchased at the store.

smallest purchases away in their carriages; they preferred to have their
parcels delivered later in the day. So it was that Harrods built up the
'carriage trade' of the leisurely rich. One assistant reported in 1890 that he
served four of the bastions of high society in one morning alone: Lady
Randolph Churchill, Baroness Schroder, the Dowager Duchess of
Manchester, and Lady Brodie.

It was about this time that Harrods began to cater for the new craze of
cycling and opened a specialist bicycle department. Cycling had become
the height of fashion by the mid-1890s, among women as well as men, and
cyclists were a common sight in Hyde Park. The store took care to
follow trends in clothing, too, often becoming a source of advice for
customers on the subject. *Hearth and Home* magazine declared, 'Harrod's
Stores is indeed a wonderful place. The outer woman can be clothed and
adorned there, whilst the inner woman can be vastly refreshed, and all her
wants can be most tastefully and economically supplied, from a brocade
dress to a tortoise-shell comb.' The store itself claimed of its footwear
department, 'The novelty, choice of style, and correctness of the offerings in

this section have developed a world-wide clientele. Everything from dainty models in gold brocade to the stoutest brogues is of the best.' How subtle is that stress on 'correctness'!

For those who lived too far away to shop at the store, residing in the country or some corner of the Empire, Harrods was by now offering a comprehensive delivery service that meant no one need be deprived of the chance of enjoying goods from the Knightsbridge emporium.

FAR LEFT AND LEFT: A 1913 promotional leaflet advertising Harrods' mail order service for 'Ladies who desire Fashions and Household Requirements stamped with the exclusiveness of the smartest London House'.

OPPOSITE: Harrods' Grand Restaurant in 1909, when it featured the Royal Red Orchestra during afternoon tea.

## AN IDEAL SPOT TO TAKE TEA

Some families of this time had sufficient inherited wealth to have no need to work, but in many of the large, new residences of the area the merchant master of the house set off early for the City. He left his wife to occupy herself as best she could – certainly not by doing any housework, as a veritable army of servants was readily available on the cheap labour market. The woman thus freed to call on friends and go shopping still wished to retain her reputation for virtue and respectability. If she was not desirous of having a chaperone, the answer was to frequent establishments of unquestionable propriety. The Harrods Grand Restaurant, and from 1911 the Rock Tea Gardens, thus became ideal spots to take tea, accompanied by the discreet strains of the Harrods Royal Red Orchestra.

For certain sections of Edwardian society, therefore, an afternoon visit to Harrods was not a mere shopping trip, but part of the social round. In 1909 Harrods could claim to be 'a recognized social rendezvous; in fact, one of the few smart rendezvous acknowledged and patronized by Society'. It

[80]

added that 'it is perfectly proper to meet a gentleman in the ground floor Banking Hall'. This was a gibe at rival store Whiteley's, whose restaurant had been cited as a 'place of assignation' in a celebrated divorce case.

1909 was the year of the great Harrods diamond jubilee celebrations, and the concerts conducted by Sir Landon Ronald and other entertainments were among the highlights of the social season. Such was the store's fame by now that it was even featured (disguised as 'Garrods') in a play,

*Our Miss Gibbs*, at the Gaiety Theatre that year, with two scenes set in reproductions of the Royal Exchange and Millinery department.

By this time the store had established its own clubs for ladies and (separately) gentlemen, where they could write letters, leave messages on an Appointments Board, or simply relax in luxurious surroundings. Even those women who were members of the most fashionable club of the time, the Alexandra Club in Grosvenor Street, could rest assured that the top people's store was but a short journey away.

In 1911 Harrods celebrated the Coronation of George V with the publication of a brochure marking its own 'coming of age', it being twenty-one years since Harrods Limited was established.

### THE HAUNT OF THE RICH AND FAMOUS

Harrods was on the crest of an elegant wave through the early years of the twentieth century, the haunt of the well-bred, rich and famous. Many of this exclusive set were on board *The Titanic* as it sailed forth on its ill-fated maiden voyage – the passenger list included ten millionaires. When the massive liner struck an iceberg off Newfoundland in April 1912, the 1,513 lives that were lost included many Harrods customers.

The same year, two windows at the store were smashed by Suffragette protestors, who are also thought to have started the fire which destroyed the Mill Lodge staff club in Barnes in 1914. Society was changing, and the onset of World War I proved a catalyst in raising the status of the female sex and later in increasing the independent spending power of middle-class women who took up newly acceptable employment. Marriage invariably signalled the end of work for a woman, Harrods staff and customers alike.

## WIDENING THE CLIENTELE

Efforts were being made, slowly, to widen the social range of customers attracted to the store, while simultaneously striving to maintain its air of refinement. Sir Woodman Burbidge realised that the store needed to recruit more regular customers to finance its expansion, and to appeal to the middle classes while retaining the local dowagers. Thus it was that Harrods allowed such promotions as a room-set of an oak-panelled Jacobean-style lounge (the word had replaced the term 'drawing room') at the Ideal Home Exhibition, which attracted a less prosperous clientele than the Knightsbridge store was used to. A new slogan, 'I *must* go to Harrods,' was introduced, and the store began running courses of instruction on dressmaking, tailoring, and French (dried) flower making to help its less-moneyed but still socially aspiring customers.

Vast numbers of people were flocking to the store by this time; on one day, more than 79,000 visitors passed through the doors. Fashion advice which had previously been dispensed on an individual basis was now offered to all potential customers, and the store began organising fashion shows to display the latest trends. In 1929 *Harrods News* advertised a talk at the store 'on resort fashion which will interest you all, because what is worn in the south now will be worn in England later in this Spring'. That same year its 'back to town' number commented, 'Returning to town at the end of summer is always rather an adventure – so much may have happened in the meanwhile. The most monstrous fashion may have been launched... there may have been a complete revolution in hats!' It went on to give some indication of the latest modes: 'Evening frocks trail to still greater lengths, day frocks will reach to four inches below the knee... gloves for formal wear will be longer and will be worn wrinkled up the forearm.'

Harrods may have been focusing on the middle classes at this time, but it continued to cultivate its image as the ultimate department store, somehow giving the impression that both store and customer were equally honoured by doing business together. The surroundings and some of the services it offered contributed to the special magic. In 1929 one could enjoy a tea dance in the luxury of the Georgian Restaurant with Victor

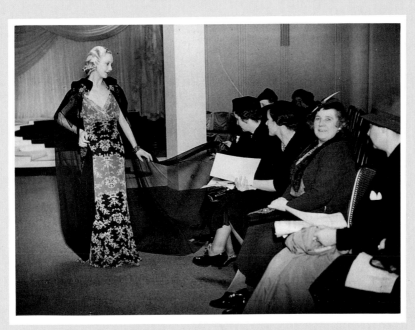

Gloria Morgan Vanderbilt models one of her dresses at a celebrated fashion
show which she staged with her twin sister Thelma, Lady Furness,
at the store in April 1937.

Silvester among the orchestra before setting off in a chauffeured
limousine hired from 6pm to midnight for 25 shillings (allowing time for
cocktails, theatre and supper).

## THE MARK OF GENTILITY

In 1935 Harrods also found an excellent way to allow customers to
capitalise on the kudos of shopping at the Knightsbridge store – the
introduction of carrier bags featuring its famous green and gold livery with
the distinctive Harrods logo. The bags were the mark of gentility wherever
they were taken, but were particularly welcomed by shoppers returning to
the growing and highly status-conscious London suburbs.

## THE LONDON SEASON

Successful as Harrods was in its efforts to widen its clientele, it was not
neglecting the upper classes. It sent staff to monitor society weddings, for
example, and it offered debutantes a wide range of services during the
London Season. The Season officially commenced with the private view at
the Royal Academy in May. It took in the racing at Newmarket, Epsom
and particularly Royal Ascot, the Henley Regatta, the Aldershot Tattoo
and a succession of coming out balls and cocktail parties in Mayfair and
Belgravia, before closing in time for a holiday in late July. Harrods was
involved at every stage – as meeting place; as supplier of clothes, accessories

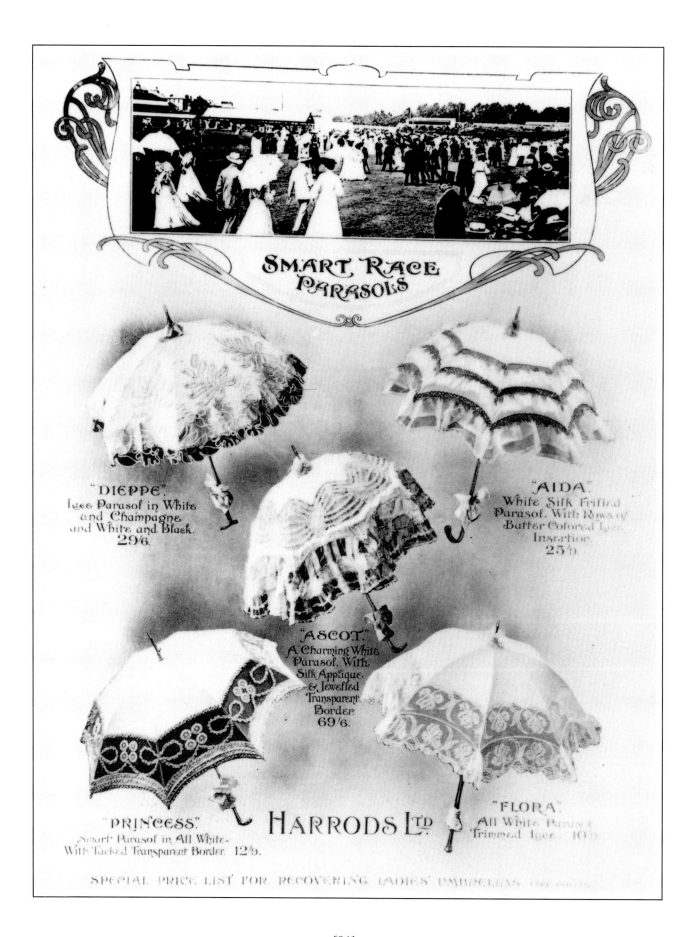

SMART RACE PARASOLS

"DIEPPE".
Lace Parasol in White
and Champagne
and White and Black.
29/6.

"AIDA".
White Silk Frilled
Parasol. With Rows of
Butter Colored Lace
Insertion.
25/9.

"ASCOT".
A Charming White
Parasol, With
Silk Applique,
& Jewelled
Transparent
Border.
69/6.

"PRINCESS".
Smart Parasol in All White
With Tucked Transparent Border. 12/9.

HARRODS Ltd

"FLORA".
All White Parasol
Trimmed lace. 10/6

SPECIAL PRICE LIST FOR RECOVERING LADIES' UMBRELLAS.

and picnic hampers for out-of-town events such as the Regatta; and as provider of chauffeured limousines in town.

An assistant who began at the store in the hot, sunny summer of 1938 recalls, 'My first impression of Harrods was its almost garden party atmosphere. The customers were either preparing for Ascot or a Presentation, and their excitement and pleasure seemed to have affected everyone at the store, so that Harrods appeared a very busy and gay place.'

## COURT PRESENTATIONS AND COMING OUT BALLS

Early in the Season the new crop of debutantes – seventeen or eighteen year-old daughters of women who had previously been presented at Court – were themselves introduced to the King at a Buckingham Palace ball. Each debutante, as her name was announced, would glide forward towards a mark on the floor, her eyes fixed on the King. Finishing off a deep curtsy with a dainty kick to keep her long dress out of the way, she moved three steps to the right to curtsy to the Queen. This procedure over, the young things were pitched into a round of dance parties and cocktails until mid July, when everyone went on holiday.

Harrods had a role to play at virtually every stage of the ritual. First, it offered a range of ball gowns at an average cost of about £12 (for those who did not have their own dressmaker to call upon), together with accessories and hairdressing facilities, all staffed by people who knew exactly what look was acceptable at Court. On the day itself, liveried servants could be hired along with the all-important limousine to sweep the party into the Palace (a service advertised in the society magazine *The Tatler*). When the event was over the Harrods Portrait Studio was available through the night to take portraits of the belle of the ball.

Closely identified with the most prestigious of society events, Harrods even helped out in the 1956 Berkeley Debutante Dress Show, when a dozen of the loveliest debutantes of the year showed a collection of British-made clothes in the Berkeley Restaurant. Harrods was on hand to help select the girls, fit the clothes, and lend its considerable expertise, the store having run fashion shows for more than a quarter of a century.

## END OF AN ERA

The last of the coming out balls was held in 1958, by which time the ritual was seen as a social anachronism. It was the end of an era for high society, signifying a shift towards more elastic social criteria. Money was becoming as acceptable as a pedigree for entry into the world of the blue-blooded. The following year, Harrods' new managing director Gordon Anthony

OPPOSITE: Earlier this century, a parasol or sun-shade – from Harrods, of course – was an essential accessory at race meetings for any lady wishing to preserve her pale complexion.

acknowledged that the store had to adjust to a changing society. 'Customers have always been intimidated by our Buckingham Palace image. They have had the idea that it costs a guinea just to walk on the carpet,' he told the influential American trade magazine *Women's Wear Daily*. 'But now we have gone to a six day week. We are making a tremendous drive for the young marrieds and we're trying to put it across that Harrods is no more expensive a place to shop than anywhere else and that at Harrods you can do it in comfort, at leisure, and get good quality.'

In fact, Harrods had for some time been offering a wider range of budget merchandise, in an attempt to attract the high-spending young people of the 1950s, but without great success. The existence of these lower-

Debutantes and their mothers relied heavily upon Harrods during the London 'Season'.

priced lines tended to be overshadowed by more sensational stories reinforcing Harrods' image as the store of the rich and famous. Even Harrods' own press officer, Isabel Newton Sharp, made the headlines when she was voted one of the best-dressed women in Britain.

## ALLIGATORS AND ELEPHANTS

Then there was the alligator bought from the store by Beatrice Lillie as a Christmas present for Noel Coward. In 1967 an elephant was purchased as a gift for California governor Ronald Reagan. Leka, self-proclaimed king of Albania, was a big Reagan fan and instructed Harrods to send fifteen-month-old 300 kg/700 lb Gertie on the long flight to San Francisco. The

The celebrated Gertie sets off on her voyage to America as a gift to Ronald Reagan from the king of Albania.

governor renamed the elephant GOP (for 'Grand Old Party', the nickname of the Republicans, whose symbol is an elephant) and disposed of the gift by donating the animal to Sacramento Zoo. But the story entered the roll of Harrods legends, setting it apart from other stores, and in a strange way, frightening away elements of the society it served.

## THE INTERNATIONAL SET

The oil boom of the 1970s, combined with Harrods' knack for attracting the custom of the seriously rich international set, led to some truly monumental spending sprees at the store, and extravagances such as a 35p handkerchief being air-freighted to Los Angeles, at a cost of £17.50.

Oil-rich Arabs became familiar customers at the store, and stories of their spending sprees abounded. In the Perfumes Hall a saleswoman piling up hundreds of pounds' worth of goods for an Arab customer was asked to stop and make up the order five times over – one set for each wife. A Saudi oil minister's £35,000 shopping list included more garden furniture than could be fitted into his limousine; a coal lorry was therefore commandeered, and the vehicles formed an unlikely convoy along the road to London's Heathrow Airport.

In fact, Harrods' clientele has become increasingly international. The store has advertised in the United States since 1920, and as far back as 1937 one staff member commented on the number of American customers. But the tourist boom that began in the 1970s and still continues today has brought an avalanche of visitors eager to see the famous store. Tours of London in a coach bearing the Harrods livery set off regularly from outside the doors of the store.

International trends have affected the development of the store itself. For example the move towards designer labels has led to the introduction of more designer concessions on the clothing floors. Here again, Harrods is holding up a mirror to society, becoming more international and yet retaining its ability to satisfy the status-conscious just by being where it is and the way it is. 'There is only one Harrods' reads the slogan – and millions of people want to boast to their friends that they have been part of it. Harrods' social cachet has gone truly global.

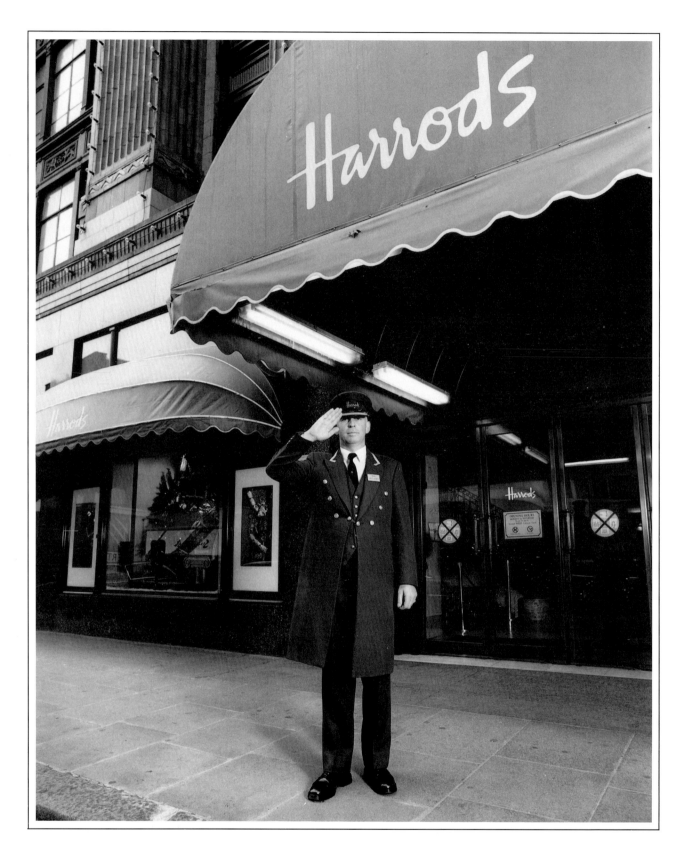

Harrods' 'Green Men' serve as ambassadors for the store and are famous for
their courtesy, tact and knowledge of Harrods and London.

# CHAPTER FIVE

# A TRADITION OF SERVICE

*Harrods*

# "Prompt and courteous response"

Harrods has always set high standards in what it sells and how it is sold. The store was late to make the shift from counter service in all goods to self service of many, because it is steeped in a culture of supplying every want of its customers, which of course requires a high degree of direct contact with them. For generations, Harrods has been able to provide anything a person might need, from the cradle to the grave. The question on the lips of the shopwalker who traditionally welcomed customers and steered them around the various departments was not so much 'Will there be anything else?' but 'What else does madam require?' – because there was always something, and it would almost certainly be in stock!

In a 1960 issue of *The Vancouver Sun* Jack Scott noted the importance of service in making Harrods such a special place:

> Where else could you order a full-dress funeral or, more happily, a full-dress wedding with the entire equipment – gowns, suits, flowers, limousines, punch for the reception and discreet counselling for the bride – all provided in one package? Yet the real pleasure of visiting Harrods, the kind of thing that causes people to roam about in it just for entertainment, has little to do with its more extravagant services. The real charm of it is that everything is done with great care, great skill, and great pride ... They will not only get you everything, as they got one customer a helicopter and another a $15,000 rhinoceros, but they'll do it with a charm and dedication that makes shopping a new venture.

## 'THE RIGHT SORT' OF STAFF

The essential raw material for such good service is good staff. Harrods has succeeded in recruiting and motivating a veritable army of 'the right sort',

The army of Harrods drivers pose proudly in their new uniforms in 1927.

who have held, and therefore perpetuated, the belief that 'there is only one Harrods' over the years. Naturally the conditions under which they work have changed with the times, too. Newcomers to the employ of Charles Digby Harrod in the 1880s were told to come in with a clean face and a clean smock at 7.30 sharp the next morning. Despite the extremely long stints they were expected to work (seventy-five hour weeks with meals taken at the counter), it was made clear that 'Mr Harrod does not employ tired staff' – so they had better not have allowed any fatigue to show!

Charles Digby Harrod ruled his workers by inspiring a blend of veneration and fear, rewarding performance with bonuses or fines, terse praise or stern admonishment as he saw fit. In fact, he was a shrewd judge of character and knew when to compromise. One Saturday evening the counter staff, who had their tea at 5pm and then worked right through to 11pm, sneaked off one by one to get refreshment. Harrod flew into a rage on discovering this unsanctioned depletion of ranks on the busiest evening of the week, but the next Saturday averted any revolt by providing a pint of beer all round at 9pm.

In addition to the penny-halfpenny fines for lateness which applied to all staff, a notice dating from 1888 reveals that despatch workers were under strict instructions not to ring any customer's doorbell after 10.30pm, on sufferance of a 2/6d fine. Anyone who arrived back at the yard later than 11pm was also penalised. Returning with an empty truck – indicating that all parcels on the round had been delivered – earned a bonus of 6d, or a shilling on the busy Saturdays.

### CLOCKING-IN DURING THE NINETEENTH CENTURY

Conditions changed markedly under the regime of Richard Burbidge, which began in 1891. He put a stop to most of his predecessor's fines and introduced a different check on lateness. Previously, entry for all staff was via a portable staircase, which Harrod would have removed five minutes before opening time, forcing latecomers to pick their shamefaced way along a route past his office! Burbidge, however, gave every staff member a numbered lead token, which they had to drop into a slotted box on their arrival for work. The box was removed precisely at 8.30am, after which time tokens had to be delivered to the timekeeper, thereby prompting a lecture on punctuality.

Burbidge also set aside time for staff to have their lunch away from their place of work. But the major change he made was one which pre-empted legislation by some time: he reduced shop opening hours immediately, and later pioneered half-day closing one day per week.

However delighted staff were at this drop in the number of hours they were expected to work, some were still prepared to try to get away with the odd deception. James Clancy, a clerk in the 1890s, tells a story of one such attempt, which was doomed to failure:

> When the Town Orders increased and we were unable to finish before closing, the Governor permitted us to take them home and bring them in next morning copied, of course, paying overtime. One very energetic man was having so much overtime that he was stopped at the door and made to untie his parcel, and the overtime consisted of 12 rashers of bacon packed between two boards and wrapped up to make the parcel look like books.

The offender was dismissed on the spot, like anyone who dared to cheat the firm. The dynamic managing director adopted an authoritarian manner which made sackings brief and conversations one-sided. But he also had a genuine desire to make his hundreds of employees feel that they were part of a family, and that Harrods formed a kind of protective roof over their heads. Staff communications of the time frequently refer to the House of Harrod, and Burbidge held Sunday bible classes for staff at his own home.

## STAFF SPORTS AND SOCIAL CLUBS

In 1894 Burbidge donated a sizeable chunk of land next to the Barnes depository for use in staff sports and social activities. Thus were born the Harrodian Club and the Harrodians Amateur Athletics Association, which offered, for a small subscription, a wide choice of activities. These became a focus for the social life of many staff. Clubs for soccer, rugby, hockey, rowing and many other sports were started, and as the clubs grew they took on a social role, with such events as annual dinners and weekend outings. Social activity had a new venue from 1904 when the splendidly equipped Mill Lodge country house and adjoining land were purchased for use by the Club. The Harrodian Club even had a club tie later on in its life: green and gold, of course, and ten shillings to members.

Woodman Burbidge (later Sir Woodman) became general manager of the growing store in 1911. He preferred to employ staff who had ambition and were not 'wasters'.

## THE HIGHEST PITCH OF EXCELLENCE

By 1911 a company brochure was able to claim:

> The highest pitch of excellence has been attained in the organization and arrangements for the welfare of the great army of assistants who are the very life-blood of the establishment... During business hours the employees are encouraged to increase their knowledge of business methods and thus qualify for promotion, and to ensure that no evils may follow the strain which falls more or less on everyone busily engaged in large commercial undertakings, every encouragement and help is given to pursuits which have for their object the mental and physical betterment of each worker.

There was a Provident Society, which received £1,000 a year from the company, and a Benevolent Fund, and staff had access to a medical officer and dental surgeon. The company had also introduced a major innovation by establishing a Staff Office, specifically responsible for engaging and managing staff. It followed this up in 1912 with the opening of a separate training department. Shortly after, a Staff Council was set up to open a channel of communication between even the most junior personnel and the management. Inspired by Richard Burbidge's son Woodman, who was now general manager, these were significant moves. They revealed a new attitude towards the staff, a recognition that employment was a two-way operation, and that investment in better staff and improved employee relations would pay off for a service-based organisation such as Harrods.

Early in 1913 the Harrodians Amateur Athletics Association had won a number of sporting trophies, and was basking in the glory of coming from behind to beat Liberty's store at football in the semi-finals of the West End Senior Cup. The win was achieved despite the absence during the first part of the match of Harrods' star forward Strike – he couldn't find the ground.

No doubt poor Strike had to endure much ribbing about the incident when he attended the Association's third annual dinner on 22 February 1913. The highlight of the occasion was a speech by Harrods' general manager Woodman Burbidge. Congratulating his audience on winning eight trophies to take their total to two dozen, he drew a moral from these efforts to apply to their working lives. 'I want you all to be as strong in your departments as you have proved to be in securing the cricket and football championships,' he said, 'and accordingly help the weak in the departments thus assisting to keep Harrods as successful in the future as they have proved to be in the past.'

Woodman Burbidge also made some revealing remarks about his criteria for staff selection: 'Personally, when engaging staff, I should give preference to a sportsman, as I would feel that I was engaging a man with ambition, and not a "waster".' Harrods had no time for 'wasters': the store was growing, and that brought promotion prospects.

## EDUCATIONAL INITIATIVES

Woodman Burbidge made it clear who would be given priority when he paid a surprise visit to the new evening classes run by Harrods. According to the new staff newspaper *The Harrodian Gazette*, launched at the beginning of 1913, his arrival in the classrooms was greeted by cheers from his employees. The paper reported that 'he emphasized that all kinds of vacancies in departments would be filled in future by those who had shown their determination to get on by attending the classes'.

Harrods was the first retailer to offer such extra education to its staff outside working hours. Perhaps it was prompted to take action by the results of the written tests on general subjects which all prospective clerical workers were now required to take. At a time when the standard and availability of basic education were erratic, the evening classes raised the quality of the store's own staff and provided an incentive to work for Harrods. The store was therefore a 'cut above' for the staff as well as for its customers.

The following year Richard Burbidge wrote to *The Times* to explain another educational initiative for its staff: 'Harrods have instituted a scheme of yearly free scholarships, which provides for training in arithmetic, handwriting, commercial English, typewriting, French or Spanish, business efficiency and salesmanship, and special training on matters purely connected with the business of the house.' Students would spend the morning in classes, work at the store in the afternoon and attend more lessons in the evenings.

The accent on improving oneself and one's knowledge of business reached as far as the *Harrodian Gazette*. It carried long, worthy essays on the origins and production of some of the world's commodities, and at one stage was even running a 'learn a phrase a day' series teaching French and Spanish. It is difficult to imagine a staff newsletter of today offering such learned and complex material to its readers.

## OPPORTUNITIES FOR WOMEN

The numbers of women sales assistants, indeed of female staff in general, had been disproportionately low early in the store's life. But the move into drapery and ladies' fashions, which demanded supervised fittings, at the end of the nineteenth century, accelerated their entry, and the shortage of male staff during World War I brought women into more departments. By 1915 the Harrodians Amateur Athletics Association was running a

Supervised fittings of ladies' fashions, introduced in late Victorian times, increased women's employment opportunities at the store.

thriving ladies' cricket section, and two years later Sir Woodman kicked off the first Harrodian ladies' football match, against munitions girls.

In August 1917 *The Harrodian Gazette* carried an article on 'the increased scope for woman as wage-earner', commenting:

> Among the many radical changes produced by the War in the lives of all sections of the community, the most striking is the rapid development of women as wage-earners in every capacity of industrial life... Gone are the prejudices and restrictions hitherto prevailing

The ladies' Wednesday Evening Physical Culture Class in 1913. By the end of World War I,
the proportion of women employed by the store had increased dramatically.

against female labour. She enters on the same footing as her brothers, and receives all the encouragement and sympathy that the most devoted parent could desire for her.

The attention was less paternal in the Despatch department, which reported, 'All the men keep a watch on the lady clerks, and if one is seen to be in any difficulty with regard to moving a parcel there is immediately a rush to help her, for we all believe in being gallant to our lady friends.'

Although women were now accepted at the workplace, their ambitions were limited. The staff training department held a debate about how men would cope with the return to civilian life after the trenches. There was general agreement that they would come to terms with women being in their places, but that buyers and other senior grades should continue to be male preserves. An exception was the store's first woman employee, Ida Fowle, who started as a clerk in 1885. By 1917 she held a very senior position in the bought ledger department with hundreds of personnel responsible to her. Her staff, known as 'Miss Fowle's chicks' were full of admiration for this determined woman who held her own in a male-dominated environment throughout her career.

## DRESS CODES FOR STAFF

Photographs of Ida Fowle show a stern, magisterial face above the regulation outfit of the day. Dress regulations for staff have changed little over the years, which is perhaps not so surprising in a conservative industry like retailing. In 1917 lady assistants were advised to wear 'neat plain black, made in good taste, and in keeping with the department they are employed in'. Stockings had to be black, and the wearing of jewellery was forbidden. These rules were extended to the behind-the-scenes clerical staff in 1923, when women were instructed to wear 'neat and becoming dark dresses'. There seems to have been some opposition to this edict, prompting a letter of support in the staff newspaper: 'May all of us who have not yet conformed to the rule remember that one or two can spoil the whole scheme, so let us try as much as we can to carry out this very reasonable regulation and then, when we do have the chance of wearing our pretties, we shall appreciate them much more.'

The one time when female staff were allowed to deviate from this uniform was when a select few were chosen to act as models in fashion shows. Harrods had used live models (departmental staff) to show individual garments since the start of the century, but soon the idea of fashion parades became popular. The chosen staff were paid nothing extra, regarding the role as an honour. From 1915, 'juvenile mannequins' (in Harrods parlance) or 'mannekids' (to the staff) joined the modelling ranks. The children were recruited from families of the staff and received a new suit in payment.

Originally male staff were expected to wear black jackets, striped trousers, and starched collars. This gradually evolved into dark grey, navy blue or black suits, and soft collars were eventually tolerated.

## DEPARTMENTAL STRUCTURE

Although they were encouraged to take an interest in the workings of the company as a whole, staff really identified far more closely with their own departments. Each department had its own operational structure, headed by the buyer, and was set individual sales targets. Promotion to another department was most unusual – career progression was much more likely to be achieved either through advancement within one department or by leaving the store altogether to join a rival shop in a higher position.

This structure developed as a reaction to the system that had prevailed under Charles Digby Harrod. At that time staff had simply worked where they were told, which was wherever the store was busiest – under Harrod the concept of building an expertise in one area of activity, of individual development, had been limited to senior staff.

Inevitably, the rigid departmental structure fostered insularity and led to rivalries and factionalism. Departments would seek, say, the best positioning in the store, or perhaps investment in new fittings. The system also grouped staff into very strong units – for example, when charabanc trips to the countryside began in 1920, they were organised on a departmental, rather than a company-wide, basis.

The exception was the Harrodian Club, which all staff were free to join, and which continued to grow as staff numbers rose with the expansion of the company's activities. An operatic section was formed in 1920 to rehearse for a production of HMS Pinafore the following Easter. (Treading the boards was a popular pastime for Harrods staff – seventeen years later, they were still applying the greasepaint and had advanced to perform at the Fortune Theatre.)

### THE MILL LODGE CLUB HOUSE

The Mill Lodge Pavilion had burnt down in 1913, and conditions there were a little spartan until its replacement was finally completed in 1929.

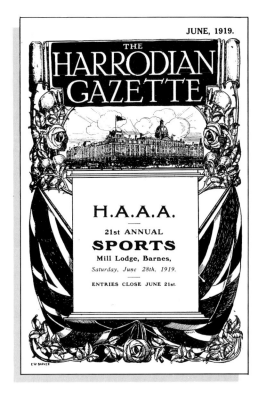

The annual sports day was a major event for
Harrods' staff and their families.

However, the Mill Lodge Club House remained in use. It featured one of the largest sprung ballrooms in London, a two-table billiard room, and numerous other social facilities. Dancing was the favoured entertainment, and there were company or departmental dances at Mill Lodge almost every Saturday night. Hours were still very long, and the work demanding, so it is no surprise that staff tended to socialise with one another – they had little time to build up much of a life outside their work.

By this time there were 20,000 children in the 'Harrod family', who were invited to compete in their own races on sports day and to devise elaborate costumes for the annual fancy dress carnival.

Sir Woodman Burbidge with his son 'Mr Richard', presenting Sir Edgar
Britten with a goodwill message to be carried on the maiden
voyage of *The Queen Mary* in 1936.

### CLEARLY DEFINED DEMARCATIONS

Just as there was a social order outside the store, inside there was a rigid
hierarchy. All three generations of the Burbidge family who ran the store
were, according to contemporary company documents, adored by the staff.
Nevertheless, all three held the power to dismiss staff at a minute's notice or
move them to a superior post. However kind, generous and fond they were
of the staff, this power alone put them on an unassailable pedestal.

They could be high-handed in their behaviour to staff, too. Ronald
Hales, who was office boy to Sir Woodman Burbidge in 1925, describes the
impatience of his employer: 'He'd press the button on his desk and he expected you in the office virtually before his finger was off it. That's what the
other boys didn't like, you wanted to be in there quick or you got barked at.'

The demarcations were just as clearly defined in 1959, when the Sir
Richard Burbidge medallion was designed by Paul Vincze to commemorate the second Sir Richard's fourteen years as chairman. Silver
versions of the coin (which featured on one side his profile and on the other
side Mercury, God of Commerce, inscribing Sir Richard's achievements on

a parchment held by the Goddess of Plenty) went to management. Buyers, who were lower down the hierarchy, had to make do with bronze.

In Sir Woodman's time, the buyers ruled their departments like feudal lords. Even wage settlements approved by the board were subtly undermined – staff received their pay from their departmental head, some of whom had no compunction about making adjustments to the amount in each pay packet. The Staff Council raised the matter in 1921 when it pointed out that there were departments who were refusing to implement the agreed new overtime rate of time-and-a-quarter for working more than the regulation forty-four-hour week.

Lowest in the hierarchy were the factory and workroom staff of Trevor Square. They were not allowed to use the Mill Lodge facilities for staff until the 1920s, having to make do instead with a worse-equipped sports club situated in Hanwell, west London.

## DRAMATIC CHANGES

Matters improved markedly when an American, Dorothy Pendleton, was put in charge of the staff training department in 1927. This remarkable woman took on the male hierarchy and pushed through a new management structure at a time when the store was having to make economies due to falling sales. She changed the rather demeaning job title 'under-the-buyer' to 'assistant buyer', and transformed the outdated methods of staff training. With better training programmes, backed up by surprise tours of inspection, she pushed up standards around the store. To encourage staff to be more alert, she would make deliberate mistakes in displays, or leave pieces of paper or string on the carpet, monitoring how long it took for them to be spotted and removed. Although she was at Harrods for only five years, she became one of its legends because of the vision, drive and common sense she brought to the job.

Doubtless she faced more battles with her fellow managers than with the staff, for few people are able to accept change without some kind of reaction. The late 1920s and early 1930s were difficult times for the store, with profits in some years falling in real terms. With the high unemployment reducing trade in 1930, Sir Woodman issued an order that all employees must take a week's unpaid leave. Harrods had pioneered paid holidays and had a reputation as a good and fair employer. But this plan would have been particularly hard on the low wage earners who formed a majority of the 7,000-strong staff. Faced with acute animosity, Sir Woodman withdrew the plan. The incident soured relationships between staff and management at the store, and rumours of redundancies swept the corridors. The *Harrodian Gazette* went so far as to itemise reasons for some of the 395 staff departures in the first six months of the year: resignations accounted for 227 of them, while there had been only 34 redundancies.

The enduring hard times did, however, lead to a cutback on overtime

The controlled frenzy of the Postal department
during the January Sale of 1932.

payments in 1932, for staff now had to work forty-eight hours in a week
before qualifying for extra reward. Some commented that the overtime
book would mysteriously disappear when the appointed time came to sign
for the extra hours! Perhaps these measures worked, for the staff turnover
rate fell from 16.5 per cent in 1927 to 12.7 per cent in 1932 – impressively
low figures for a notoriously transient occupation such as shop work.

## UNDER THE BANNER OF THE HOUSE

Sir Richard Burbidge had fostered a collective pride in the store and in
service which did much to enhance Harrods' reputation. When he died in
1917 his son Sir Woodman said in a letter to staff: 'To my Fellow-Workers.
On behalf of my family and myself, I should like to express our deep
gratitude for your generous support and sympathy in our great bereave-
ment. You have shown us so clearly that our loss is your loss, that you have
made my father's dream of being one united family a wonderful reality.'
The same sentiments are evident in this extract from a 1930 issue of the
*Harrodian Gazette*: 'It is an honourable record to be identified for so long a
period with the fortunes of one Firm. To feel that you have done your part
in building up its name and reputation. To have shared its trials and
success. And if fortune has not come your way, it has at least enabled you,
in many cases, to bring up a family in comfort, many of whom in their turn
have taken their place under the banner of the House.'

Indeed there were many large families who were sustained 'under the banner of the house'. There were even some in which every working member was on the Harrods payroll. Many were in attendance at a huge party in the Albert Hall on 14 March 1935. The event celebrated Sir Woodman Burbidge's forty years with the company; he had stood down as managing director in 1931 to be replaced by his son, Richard, but had retained the role of chairman. He was presented with a casket containing the name of every employee, after which there was dancing to 'Gordon Marsh and his Silver Jubilee Cabaret'.

## THE COMMISSION SYSTEM

Not all staff found the patriarchal working of Harrods to their liking. The commission system, under which staff were paid a basic wage plus a commission based on how much they sold, attracted criticism. A woman assistant wrote in 1930, 'The commission system is thoroughly pernicious and should be abolished. It fosters a spirit of envy, hatred and greed,' adding, 'the antics of a commissioned assistant with a customer remind me of a dog with a bone.' She also gave some indication of the tensions between rival assistants: 'If the poor wretch moves two or three feet in any direction she is poaching on someone else's preserves and she is not allowed to forget the fact for many a day to come.' In fact, at the time Harrods was paying a higher basic wage than most of its rivals, and offering less in commission. It did not want to encourage the pestering of customers by over-enthusiatic sales assistants, as this would detract from the atmosphere of genteel decorum in the store. Harrods, like many other retailers, believes the system works, for many sales staff today are still paid partly in commission.

Another member of staff wrote complaining about the patronising attitude of management to staff, embodied in the staff newspaper: 'I feel sure that if you start by assuming that we are not clock watchers, nor idlers, nor duffers, you will achieve more actual good,' wrote Percy Collas, who appropriately enough honed his writing skills in the Correspondence office. He suggested that management attitudes were stuck in a 'snobbish, unctuous' past, and that 'the Harrodian of today is a different type of chap from his Victorian prototype'. The Editor responded with a pithy 'pity you have got that Red Flag bee in your bonnet'.

## CONDITIONS OF SERVICE

Nevertheless, the company was stung by the comments because it believed, rightly, that it offered some of the best conditions in the retail market. It was particularly proud of the pension scheme (even though in 1932 the entry point was raised from fifteen to twenty years' service), and all Harrodian pensioners received a generous Christmas hamper. No doubt this whetted their appetites for a return to the hustle and bustle of the store as temporary staff for the January Sale.

The ladies' staff rest room had an atmosphere of decorum.
This photograph dates from around 1948.

Long service was rewarded in holiday entitlement too. From the 1930s until at least the late 1950s this consisted of two weeks' paid leave plus a spring holiday of three days (or five Saturday mornings), upon completion of a full year's unbroken service. A decade of service earned the right to take these three days plus the five Saturday mornings, and after twenty years with the company the extra leave was six days plus the Saturdays off.

Although such allowances seem small to our modern eyes, the conditions of employment at Harrods were the best in the industry at the time. Harrods continued to stay ahead by introducing benefits such as sick pay to keep its reputation for being the cream of retail employers. The trade paper *Draper's Record* was to comment that the second Sir Richard Burbidge had done more than any other man to improve standards of personnel welfare in retailing.

## A GREAT ARMY OF EMPLOYEES

As a major store in its own right, within a group of satellite retailers, Harrods became a large-scale employer. During the reign of the first Sir Richard Burbidge, staff numbers rose from 400 in 1890 to 6,000 in 1913. The figure had reached 7,000 by 1939 (more than the store employs today), but not all worked on the shop floor: 3,000 were in sales, packing and despatch, 2,000 in the workrooms and 1,000 in accounts, advertising and secretarial work, while the remaining 1,000 were occupied in miscellaneous activities such as running the huge staff restaurant. (A new one had opened

Behind the scenes at Harrods. TOP: Part of the busy factory in Trevor Square. This is the Silver and Electro Plating Finishing Shop in 1929. ABOVE: Aided by extremely efficient delivery and postal systems, what the Despatch department packed in the morning was often with the customer the same day.

in 1930 sporting 250 tables in neat rows with four chairs at each – the very model of the modern canteen.)

The army of backroom factory workers, based mainly in the Trevor Square building, included highly skilled craftsmen. Until the 1970s, production of many Harrods own-brand goods, as well as all repairs, was undertaken by people on the firm's payroll. The workforce included chocolate makers, tea blenders, silversmiths, lace workers, watchmakers and trunk makers, to name but a few.

## ACCOUNT CUSTOMERS

The quality of the goods such craftsmen made provided an extra incentive for regular customers to take out an account with the store. Since the day Charles Digby Harrod lifted the ban on credit, the store has amassed an army of account customers. By 1925, 80 per cent of store business was done on credit, and the accounts department was sending out 130,000 statements a month. Today there are 200,000 account customers.

In many ways the growing band of account customers has been the backbone of Harrods' success. They provide the regular custom that comes with the convenience of merely quoting a number over the counter or the telephone. (At first, however, security of account customers' names was lax; some fraudsters became adept at overhearing the clients' names, and then promptly using that name to buy expensive goods around the rest of the store!)

In 1909 Harrods claimed it had pioneered telephone shopping, and such was its success that it extended the service to allow telephone ordering

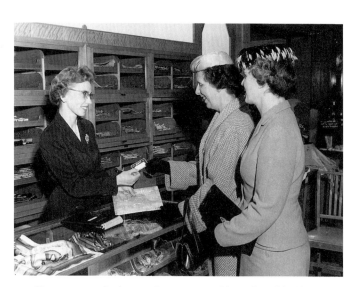

Customers study the novel account card introduced in 1957.

twenty-four hours a day. You can still order goods by telephone from Harrods at any hour of the day or night. The phones were manned round the clock until 1972, when the night shift was replaced by a pair of answering machines. (The second machine was introduced after a customer fell asleep while dictating an order, and filled a whole tape with snoring!)

## HARRODS NEWS

Harrods has taken care to keep account and other potential customers informed of its range of products over the years. In 1917 it began regular publication of *Harrods News*. Containing details and prices of new and

The pioneering telephone order room in 1909.

noteworthy goods, it replaced a more comprehensive annual catalogue that had detailed every item Harrods sold. *Harrods News* was sent to 15,000 homes in London alone, and was available free to anyone who cared to ask for it, evolving into something rather like a woman's magazine. Orders could be made in person, sent by post or telephoned to the store. *Harrods News* helped to create a national, and indeed international, market for the store's products.

During the 1960s it divided into a number of separate departmental issues, and since 1981 the store has published its own upmarket glossy magazine for account customers.

## THE HARRODS FLEET

The growing market for Harrods' goods inevitably led to the expansion of the Despatch department from its humble origins as a couple of hand carts pushed round the streets of Knightsbridge. 1886 saw the investment in the first horse and cart, and in 1893 Harrods made its first long-distance suburban delivery run. A horse drew a two-wheel cart from Sloane Street to Crystal Palace in south London, and after an hour's grazing was hitched up to trot back to the store via Dulwich. Such was the route three times a week, with a different direction being taken the other three days, leaving Sundays to recover in the company stables. These stables soon required enlargement. In 1895 the company purchased seventeen horses at about forty guineas each. Four years later the delivery rounds had grown so much that Harrods bought that number in one month alone, in a year when the

Some of the famous Harrods delivery fleet through the years. TOP: The horse-drawn carts of 1896. ABOVE: The new motor fleet outside the store in 1907. LEFT: A van used solely for bread deliveries on local routes in the 1920s.

stable increased by forty. Harrods was renowned for the fine horses which it used on its delivery rounds and hired out to customers, and in 1909 111 horses were purchased to meet the rising demand.

At around this time seventy-five clerks visited homes in a two-mile radius of the store every morning to take orders, arranging delivery by 2pm that day. Another 200 clerks opened the post at 6am to put yet more orders into the system.

By now, however, the Wheelwrights department had become the Motor Maintenance department, for early in the century Harrods took up with the new-fangled motor car. Six were in use by 1903, clattering along the roads with their steel tyres. They broke down frequently, and the drivers, mostly ex-hansom cab men, relied on an Austrian mechanic to keep the vehicles on the road.

The notices posted on the walls for drivers and porters made it clear that their standards must be kept high at all times, too. Staff had to be clean and smart (caps issued free, leather uniforms available at half price) and were expected to start work promptly at 7am. Smoking while on duty was a serious offence, and being caught twice brought the sack. If a vehicle broke down and the driver could not get to a telephone, he was to telegraph his plight to the famous address 'Everything, London'.

The Despatch department was eventually split into a town section and a suburban section as it widened its delivery area. As early as 1919 Harrods had launched, with a fanfare in *Harrods News*, four deliveries a day in the local area as far away as Pimlico, with three visits to Bayswater and two daily to Hampstead. Over the years it expanded and (less publicly) shrunk the service, which at one time included a run down to Brighton. This was in addition to the thriving Harrods Removals section which would transport furnishings across the world. Its bulky, heavy lorries were so slow that trips down to Devon took several days. (The drivers used to cook steak in the engine en route, bringing a different meaning to the phrase 'meals on wheels'!)

Clearly it required a major workforce with logistical backup to maintain such a comprehensive and immediate service. Statistics available for 1922 show that the company delivered 25,000 parcels carried on the last twelve of its horse-drawn vans, with the bulk of the loads going in a fleet of ninety petrol vans and seventy electric vans. The growth of Harrods' furniture removals business added to demand, and fifteen years later the fleet had doubled to 320 vehicles, all decked out in the green and gold Harrods livery, and all serviced where they had been assembled in the Harrods depot.

A 1938 Harrods delivery van.

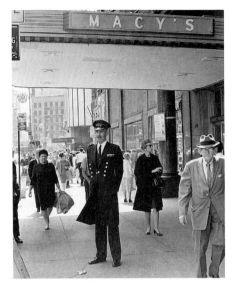

Green Men have been part of Harrods since 1909. LEFT: One of these ever-polite commissionaires helps a customer into a cab. RIGHT: William Weaver, in the right uniform at the wrong store – he went to Macy's in New York as part of a Harrods promotion in 1968.

The electric vans (called Walker vans because the engine and chassis came from the American firm of that name) were famous for their quiet efficiency in making round trips of sixty miles a day before their nightly recharge. Two are still in existence: one at the Science Museum not far from the store, the other at the Beaulieu Motor Museum in Hampshire. Early models had no windscreens, so in bad weather a driver would stretch a piece of canvas across the front, and peer out to see as best he could.

Today Harrods has a fleet of about forty vehicles making up to 7,000 delivery runs a week within a 32-kilometre/20-mile radius of the store. It has also reintroduced the horse-drawn cart service for local deliveries.

## THE GREEN MEN

Some of the best-known and most easily recognised staff of this famous store are the commissionaires who man its entrances. 'Green Men', as they are known because of their splendid uniforms, were once required to be a minimum of 190 cm/6 foot 3 inches tall. Even though this is not essential today, they must combine an encyclopedic knowledge of the store and how to get about London with the diplomatic skills of an ambassador. The store's battalion of old, rich and sometimes distinctly eccentric customers are among the many who are escorted into the store from their limousines by these statuesque commissionaires. The Green Man stationed at Door 7 alone hails 300 taxis a day. Listening in on their dealings with customers and passers-by for even a few minutes leaves one astonished at their tact, memory and patience.

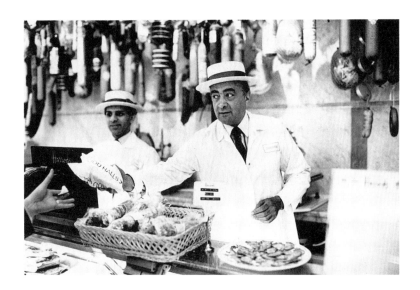

Harrods chairman Mohamed Al Fayed likes to patrol the shop
floor. Here he goes a step further and appears behind the
delicatessen counter to serve a customer.

## THE HARRODS WAY

Since 1988 people looking for employment at Harrods have been directed
to the personnel department on the fifth floor. This busy department
interviews 12,000 potential staff per year from about 25,000 job enquiries.
At almost any time of the day a handful of nervous applicants will be filling
in forms and awaiting a preliminary interview – the store is a beacon for
job hunters.

Harrods today employs 4,000 staff, with an extra 1,000 at Sale and
Christmas time, and runs six in-house training schemes. The staff employed
by the various concession outlets within the store are additional to this
figure, probably taking it nearer 5,000. With retailing more competitive
than ever, Harrods works hard to keep its standards of service high, and all
staff go through the 'Harrods Way' company customer care programme
early in their time at the store. They have a lot to cope with, beyond just
learning their way around.

One of the more unusual tasks the staff have collectively performed
was to help a blind woman learn her path through the shop. 'I have been
blind for the last twelve months,' she wrote to the store, 'and when I
returned to London I began to use your store to teach myself to walk round
without help, learning to sense solids and spaces and people without
crashing into anything.' Like many letters the company has received over
the years, the woman commented on the staff's kindness, patience and
help. There are no better tributes a store receives than letters bearing such
sentiments, and Harrods has had more than its share in its time.

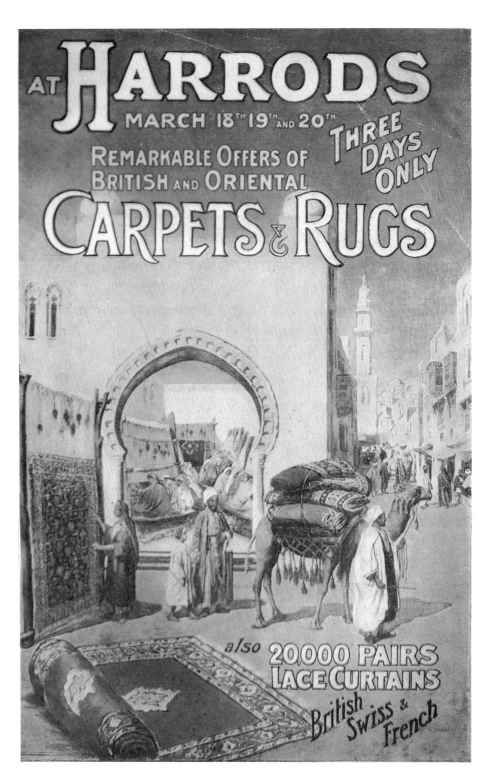

A 1912 advertisement which bears out Harrods' motto
of 'Everything for Everybody Everywhere'.

# CHAPTER SIX

## THE DEPARTMENTS

—— *Harrods* ——

# "Everything for Everybody Everywhere"

Harrods is famous for the range of goods it offers, and for its willingness to go out of its way to find unusual items: if somebody wants it, Harrods will supply it. The Harrods of 1884 boasted eighty departments. Today the figure is about 300. In the intervening century, departments have been created, moved and, in some cases, closed as the store reflects the ebb and flow of demand in the many markets it serves.

### A TOUR OF THE VICTORIAN STORE

An astonishingly rapid pace of change has been sustained since the rebuilt store opened in 1884. Where Harrods has felt a need could be met, or indeed a new market created, in has come a fresh department; and if that product's star fades, a new trend is allowed to replace it. The 1884 store was a different being entirely from the humble grocers of thirty years before – in fact, the only thing it had in common with its predecessor was the address. The local *Chelsea Herald* newspaper devoted several columns to describing the newcomer. Inspired both by the impressive scale of the shop, and the boldness of Charles Harrod in so resolutely recovering from the disastrous fire the previous Christmas, the newspaper described the store as follows:

> As we enter from the street we are struck by the vast area that opens to
> our view, but we proceed at once to the basement and here we find
> strong rooms where the silver goods kept in stock can be placed safely
> after closing hours; here too cellars built purposely for the storing of
> sugar, others for provisions, and bins by the score for the various
> assortment of wines and spirits. There are also tea rooms piled up with

[111]

Coffee was one of the earliest products sold by Harrods.
This coffee pack is from the early 1900s.

chests, from the lowly 'mixed at two shillings per pound' to the aristocratic 'scented pekoe', and another 'all the sweet perfumes of Arabia' containing the spices and other condiments of an appetizing nature.

Ascending, we are in the 'shop', and in the centre we see a large circular counter where orders are to be written out and instructions given to a staff of clerks specially appointed for the purpose. On the left there are the wines, and we find a stock assorted to suit the taste of all opponents of total abstinence. There are clarets from 'ordinaire' to high class Chateau productions, ports of the vintages sacred to those who have no dread of the gout, and selected from the best shipments of Cockburn, Kopke, Graham, Morgan and others. Champagnes from that bearing the very broad description 'superior' up to such luxurious drinks as Giesler, Mumm, Perinet, Piper or Pommery, while for those of smaller means or semi-abstainers there are the exhilarating but somewhat saccharine liquors that owe their origin to fruits grown on British soil. Then there are spirits called not 'from the vasty deep' – for water is a matter that when Gin, Brandy, Rum or Whisky are concerned Mr Harrod prefers to leave to the discretion of his customers – but there are those of the mineral class of soda from the medicinal Carlsbad, Schlossbunnen, Taunas and some which are surely bottled for the fair sex, namely, Mesdames and Celestines.

Stretching from here for a long way into the distance is the tea and grocery counter where pyramids of tea and sugar, mountains of coffee are mixed up with tins of biscuits, breeches' paste, blancmange, glycerine, lobsters, plate powder, sugar candy, boot top powder, wax vestas, salt, prawns, phosphor paste, oysters, milk, knife polish, house flannel, dog biscuits, mustard and a thousand and one other articles of a heterogeneous nature, but all of which meet in the store room of any well ordered household.

Next on the right come the fruit and flower department and here is to be a collection that will hold its own against any of the Covent Garden shops, while the flowers there are to be daily supplies of shrubs and blooming plants, nor are the beaux' and belles' requirements in the shape of bouquets and 'buttonholes' to be forgotten.

Beyond this is the 'stall' where poultry and game are to be on view, and we are informed that arrangements have been made for a constant and daily supply direct from the country so that the handling, packing and repacking which is so objectionable but which it is impossible to prevent with ordinary market-bought produce will be entirely avoided, and to complete this side of the place there is a long counter where cheeses from America, the foreign Gruyere, Chapzugar, Camembert and the delicious productions of Wilts are to be found. Here too will be seen the goods comprised under the heading 'general provisions', such as Australian meats, bacon, butter – not bosch – and hams from York, Ireland, Canada, or Westphalia.

As we look around this ground floor we are quite surprised at the enormous quantities of each article that it appears necessary to keep ready, but it is explained that often, and more particularly at holiday times and on Saturdays, there is such a rush of customers that unless this precaution was taken it would be impossible to serve quickly enough to keep the place even moderately clear.

In the middle of this floor is a grand staircase wide enough for five or six persons to ascend or descend abreast and this takes us to a spacious warehouse where we find an amazing show of sterling silver and electro goods, and being all perfectly new and freshly unpacked the effect is somewhat more than one would expect to find in any retail establishment of ordinary dimensions.

There are spoons and forks of all sorts, tea services, trays, biscuit boxes, soup tureens, kettles and stands, but a very noticeable feature is a splendid assortment of the goods that are now somewhat the rage, namely jugs, flagons, salad bowls, trays, etc. made of oak and mounted in electro. These of themselves are worth seeing, and will, we doubt not, attract a good many people to lounge on this floor. . . . there is a big show of lamps, from those burning benzoline and costing a few pence, to the delicately painted china varieties, for the drawing room or boudoir, and as a direct contrast there are lanterns for stable use and the burglar's bull's-eye.

Around the wall are cases for saddlery, and the stock comprises everything from the donkey's pad to the racing saddle, or from the halter to a set of four-horse harness, while further on there are boxes, portmanteaux, overland trunks, hat cases, in fact travelling luxuries of every conceivable shape and size. To the left there are the modern brass goods comprising high class fenders, fire irons, coal boxes, and beyond are kitchen requisites and turnery, mats, brushes, etc. The whole of this spacious floor is under the management of Mr Smart, and he is to be congratulated on having produced a show that, being almost unique in this class of business, deserves to be fully patronized by all who visit his employer's new premises.

One flight higher and we are in a portion of the building that is sure to find favour with the gentler sex, for here are displayed all sorts of fancy requisites for the toilet, perfumes from the laboratories of

Harrods in Edwardian times. The store has always prided itself
on the elegance of its entrances, stairways, lifts and corridors
as well as the departments.

Atkinson, Piesse, and Rimmel, together with the countless odds and ends in the way of cosmetiques that are eagerly sought after by those who indulge in 'paint, powder and patches'. Then comes a stock of articles equally or even more necessary, but not quite so much sought after, namely patent medicines, and arrangements have been perfected with a competent dispenser in the neighbourhood so that prescriptions at store prices can be made up without delay.

After all this realism, turning to something of a lighter character we find ourselves surrounded by games of all sorts – croquet, billiards, chess boards and the racing game, and another bearing the somewhat wild title of 'Go-bang'. There are also coupelette, magic skittles, tareteer, la poule, knock-em-downs, and last, the dear old soul for whom we have such affection at holiday times, 'Old Aunt Sally'.

On the third floor we find iron and brass bedsteads and bedding suited for high, low, rich or poor, but on the way down we pass through a pair of iron doors to find ourselves in an immense place set apart for the exhibition of furniture, and thence into a huge reserve store of all the goods that are in daily requisition in the different departments.

Descending once more we are shown over the stables, where there are stalls and loose boxes for a large number of horses, together with standing room for carts, vans and hand trucks in endless variety: and with this our tour of inspection ends.

## SERVICES OFFERED BY EDWARDIAN HARRODS

In 1904, twenty years after the *Chelsea Herald* report, an early Harrods catalogue enumerated the range of services the shop now offered:

Things you can do at Harrods besides shopping. You can insure your life and property... buy, sell and let your House or Estate... buy or sell stocks and shares... rent a safe deposit... bank on deposit or current account.

You can book your stall for the theatre... your ticket for a railway journey...your berth for a voyage... your goods or chattels to any part of the world. You can get your hair dressed... hire a carriage... lunch or dine on the premises... warehouse your furniture and household effects... advertise in any paper... and store your furs, tapestries, etc.

## A TOUR OF THE MODERN STORE

The services, and departments, have been increasing ever since. A full tour of the store today in the manner of the *Chelsea Herald* would take at least a couple of hours. You would begin at any of twelve entrances and progress via fifty lifts and four banks of escalators. Given the intricate layout of the building, the unfamiliar customer is bound to suffer a few lost bearings on the way, but is guaranteed to find much that delights and surprises.

The entrances to the store are all at ground floor level, which is generally the busiest area of the shop. Here the senses are excited first by the mingling fragrances of the Perfumes Hall, then by the wonderful aromas of the Food Halls. Harrods is the only department store that did not start life as a draper's and the ground floor conjures up its origins as a grocer's in the most evocative way. Fresh bread, innumerable cheeses and seafoods combine into a heady mixture as you wander through these high-ceilinged palaces. No visitor to Harrods should neglect the Food Halls. They provide a sense of the magnificence of Harrods' past, which has been carefully

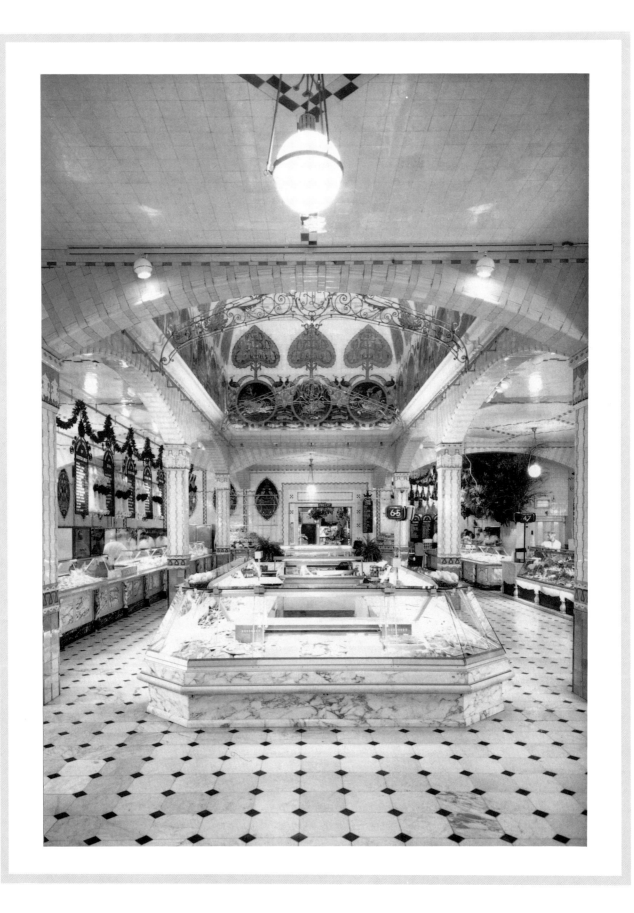

preserved or re-created today, producing an impression of effortless style. From the cool air of the Floral Hall, to the Charcuterie with its ranks of salamis and hams on one side, faced by an equally impressive array of cheeses on the opposite wall; from the mirrored arches, coloured tiles and embossed cornices of the Bakery to the artistic fish display glistening on its special stand, there is much to please the senses. And that does not even take into account the Confectionery Hall, or the Pantry on the floor below, both of which would tempt a saint.

The ground floor is a floor for both luxuries and necessities. Apart from the astonishing arrays of foods and perfumes, there are clocks and watches, gifts and jewellery, silver and plate, fashion accessories and cosmetics, leather goods and stationery, and men's clothing of all kinds. (It was for years a truism throughout retailing that men refuse to climb to upper floors to look at clothes!) If you need the bank, hairdressing, or theatre or travel tickets, all are on offer on the floor below. The basement is being redeveloped to provide extra selling space.

The first floor has more of the look of a traditional department store. Here can be found huge ranges of ladies' fashions (at least 8,000 dresses are available at any time), shoes, bridal wear, and clothes for children, amid an atmosphere of considerably greater tranquillity than the floor below.

Ascend whichever way you choose, but make sure you do not miss the second floor at Harrods, for it offers the greatest variety of any floor and is a must for anyone wishing to savour Harrods at its most comprehensive. It is a place of contrasts. There is the unhurried elegance of the China and Crystal sections, and the equally ordered but far more frenetic Books department. Leave the large-screen television sets in the Radio and Television area and you pass through the Pet Shop, where a corgi may be chasing a red ball across the floor. Continue through to the serenity of Dress Fabrics, with its large swathes of expensive cloth, expertly measured and sliced. The second floor is bursting with items for the home, such as lighting and linens, kitchen furniture and cookers, typewriters and table mats.

There are many more furnishings, including antiques, beds, baths, and carpets, on the wide expanses of the third floor, where customers can choose from the 350 different suites of furniture on show.

The scene livens up considerably on the fourth floor, which Harrods has long set aside for the younger set. There is the matt black and metal elegance of the Way In boutique, other young fashions, nursery furniture, and, of course, the famous Toy department. Here you may find a gang of children noisily urging on a friend playing pinball, not far from a tiny girl

OPPOSITE: The spectacularly refurbished Meat Hall in 1989. In the centre of the ceiling is one of the original light wells.

engrossed in a puzzle, while behind her a baffled crowd gathers around a card trick demonstration. A six-foot teddy bear in a Harrods 'Green Man' uniform imperiously studies the scene. Alive with noise and movement, the Toy section is as boisterous and exciting as any child could wish.

The fifth floor houses the enormous Olympic Way sports complex, relocated from the floor below, and carrying equipment and accessories for every conceivable sport. Croquet sets mingle with baseball hats, leather saddles stand imperiously by nets cushioning speeding squash balls struck by experimenting customers.

Dotted throughout this emporium are restaurants, bars, toilets, and service departments such as dry cleaning, lighter repairs and export. The variety is stunning, and the complexity of keeping the whole show operating smoothly is formidable. It would take an encyclopedia to describe the fortunes of the various departments over the last century, but here is an A–Z of highlights of Harrods' past, present and future.

## ANTIQUE MAPS AND PRINTS

A is for the Antique Maps and Prints department, which opened on the fourth floor in 1977 with a range of more than 20,000 items at least a century old, all framed and mounted. (The department has since been redesignated Old Maps and Prints.)

## AEROPLANES

A is also for Aeroplanes, which Harrods began to sell in 1919 – right at the start of the aeroplane boom – and again from 1930. (Yes, they did winch a plane on to the second floor – it was a Gipsy Moth.)

## ART GALLERY

A stands too for the recently opened Art Gallery, which specialises in fine and applied art by contemporary British painters, and forms part of a complete complex offering everything from posters to fine art. The first serious art gallery to inhabit a department store, it holds a regular schedule of exhibitions.

## BANKING HALL

B is for Banking Hall, which offers a service begun in 1890. From the start of this century it has provided facilities for banking plus writing and making telephone calls. It was, in fact, a popular meeting place: businessmen, relatives, friends and lovers have used the Harrods Banking Hall as their point of contact over the decades. Here the butlers and housekeepers of the grand local establishments came to settle their accounts, queueing at the edge of its palatial foyer. Harrods set up its own bank in 1893, with three employees. By 1930 it had a staff of thirty-three and held 300,000 current accounts. A new Banking Hall, which looked

The Bank counter in 1922 – note the highly ornate ironwork.

more like a spacious hotel foyer with its vast floor dotted with armchairs, was unveiled in 1936 and survived into the 1970s, when the facility was transferred to the fourth floor. In 1988 the renamed Harrods Bank Limited, providing a full banking service six days a week, opened in its new Banking Hall in the basement.

## BOOKSELLING AND BOOKBINDING

B is also for the Books department which first opened its doors in 1905 and still offers a wide selection of books. Bookbinding was offered as early as 1900. In 1913 the Harrods bookbinders working in Trevor Square earned the dubious honour of having the lowest sales of any department in the store, with a total value of £4. They did not survive for long!

## CHINA AND GLASS

C is for China and Glass. This department covered 2,000 square metres/ half an acre in 1919, and claimed to offer 'the most beautiful selections of

The China and Glass department in 1909, when Harrods boasted of it: 'A
well arranged and beautiful department which cannot fail to elicit admiration.
The orderly placing of such immense varieties reflects the deft handling
of masterly system and organisation.' The sentiment holds true today.

China, including examples of such celebrated ware as Minton, Doulton,
Wedgwood, Crown Derby, Brown Westhead, Coalport, Limoges and
Dresden'. Many of these names are still featured on the vast stock of this
section, which holds 700 ranges at any one time. At Sale time, it is a
familiar sight on the television News, as throngs of customers lean over
precarious and expensive heaps of china to pluck out their bargains.

## CLOCKS

C stands too for Clockwinding, which was another unusual service offered
by Harrods. It used to undertake yearly contracts to regulate and wind
clocks within a five kilometre/three-mile radius of the store.

## CLUBS AND CATERING

C is also for the Ladies' Club and Gentlemen's Club, which were such
popular meeting places in the Edwardian era; and for Harrods' Catering
service, which can set up a private cocktail party for a dozen people or a
formal dinner for a thousand.

Harrods' Edwardian Dress Salons were renowned throughout Europe. This is the
Costume department in 1909, forming the entrance to the Drapery
and Fashion sections. The first floor has been a centre for ladies'
fashion throughout this century.

### DRESS SALONS

D is for the elegant Dress Salons of Edwardian times, which were
considered the finest in Europe. In opulent surroundings models would
roam the salon wearing some of the clothes for sale, and customers wishing
to try on the garments were ushered into luxurious fitting rooms. The
gowns themselves were a splendid array of special versions of the latest
fashions – Harrods claimed in 1911 that its 'great forte lies in adapting
Continental creations to English tastes and conditions'.

### DECORATING

D is also for Decorating and home improvements. In the 1920s Harrods
advertised to its customers that it could carry out alterations, decorations,
sanitation, electric wiring, heating, and installation of bells and telephones.

### ESTATES OFFICE

E is for the Estates Office. With its location at the very heart of one of
London's most expensive and sought-after areas, Harrods is ideally situated

to act as agents for sales of property. The department began life tucked behind Furnishings in 1897, but by 1920 the Estates Office had grown sufficiently to open up its auction rooms. These were seen as a barometer of the property market until they were destroyed by a bomb in World War II. Between 1923 and 1929 the Estates Office doubled its turnover, having sold 456 properties. To this day, shoppers come across displays of local properties on the market, as the estate agency within the store continues to thrive from the Banking Hall, along with its Park Lane head office.

## EXPORTS

E is also for the Exports department. Catering as it does for an increasingly international clientele, Harrods has built up a remarkable export trade which accounts for about one-fifth of all purchases. In 1984 the store won a Queen's Award for Export Achievement.

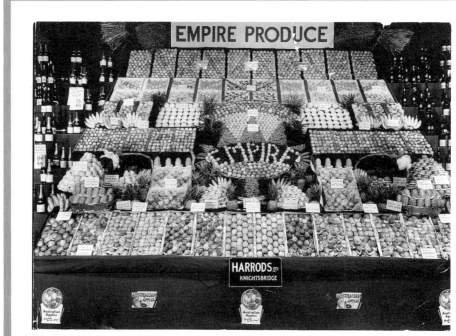

The Food Halls have a tradition of superb displays. This array was painstakingly assembled for a show of Empire produce in 1934.

## THE FOOD HALLS

F is for three of the mainstays of Harrods' business throughout its history, the first being Food. The store began its life selling non-perishables such as tea, but under Charles Digby Harrod it began offering fruit and vegetables and soon gained a reputation as a supplier of top-quality produce. The first of the Food Halls were built in 1901, and customers were startled at the opulence of the decoration, with frescoes on the ceilings and beautifully coloured tiles on the walls.

The Food Halls were largely rebuilt in 1971 to cover 557 square metres/6,000 square feet, offering groceries, coffee, tea, frozen foods, charcuterie and dairy produce, flowers and fruit. Twelve years later an enlarged Pantry was opened at basement level, to provide the best in self-service shopping. A demonstration area and an elegantly decorated coffee counter were also introduced. Up on the ground floor, a new Confectionery department opened, the delectable offerings nicely set off by the marble flooring: today customers purchase 100 tons of chocolate per year.

In October 1983 Her Royal Highness Princess Anne officially opened the further-extended Food Halls following a £2.6 million project which increased their total size to seventeen departments in seven halls, covering 4,180 square metres/45,000 square feet. The Bakery was restored to its 1903 glory, a street entrance (from Door 11) was finally built and two new restaurants added. The following year the Fruit and Vegetable Hall was also redeveloped as part of the huge rebuilding project in this department. The range of goods offered in the Harrods Food Halls is incredible: 500 different cheeses, 130 types of bread, and fresh strawberries all year long.

### FURNITURE

F is also for Furniture, another important department within Harrods for many years. Always among the top ten on the sales chart, it sometimes overtakes the Food and Fashion departments to become the highest revenue spinner.

Just after World War I the department held its first auction, and in November 1958 the hammer was in action for the one-thousandth sale. In the meantime the auctions had been transferred from their original location in Trevor Square. When that part of the building was demolished a store of guns and pistols was discovered under the floorboards – it turned out to be unsold stock hidden away by auction staff who could not think of a better way of disposing of the unwanted items!

One of the most extraordinary pieces of furniture the store has seen was sold in 1975. It was a four-poster bed, with a canopy made to match the customer's bedroom wall, 3 metres/10 feet long, 3.7 metres/12 feet wide, and 2 metres/7 feet high. Built into the bed was a quadraphonic radio, cassette deck and turntable, radio alarm clock, pop-up colour television, coffee percolator, cocktail cabinet and refrigerator. The sheets were designed by Pierre Cardin. The price of this bizarre concoction was £8,298.

The demands on space that furniture makes became something of a joke among staff. In 1932, in a lighthearted look at what the store would be like 100 years on, 'The Seer' wrote for the *Harrodian Gazette*: 'Staff and public are once more warned not to attempt the crossing of the Furniture Department without a competent guide. Yesterday a search party

In 1919, when this photograph was taken, the Ladies' Outfitting department
was re-christened Evening and After Six. The spacious setting was unchanged.

discovered a customer reported missing for two days in the Bedstead
Section. He was in the last stages of exhaustion, and said he had not seen a
human being for 48 hours.'

## FASHION

Finally, F is for Fashion. Harrods' customers love fashion, and the store has
endeavoured to offer the latest in style since it began stocking clothing at
the end of the last century. A 1918 Harrods fashion leaflet claimed that the
store 'offers at least twice as large a selection as is to be found in any other
House in Britain.' The women's magazine *The Sphere* gave its vote of
confidence to a Harrods innovation the following year:

> In these days of expensive clothes it is indeed a boon and a blessing to
> know where one can get really chic frocks for day or evening at pre-war
> prices... Harrods have opened a new department in which these may
> be found in endless and charming variety – where no gown costs more
> than 5 1/2 guineas... This new department offers an unlooked-for
> opportunity to the woman with a modest dress allowance and fastidious
> taste to possess herself of dainty frocks for all occasions.

Such was Harrods' reputation in the fashion industry that, in 1974,

WF Loudon, first floor divisional manager, received a prestigious French award, the first time it had been given in the UK. The Salon International du Prêt à Porter Feminin awarded him its coveted Golden Pin for best contribution to the promotion of French fashion.

Clothing departments have been and gone almost as fast as the changing fashions over the years, but the story of the Fur Salon encapsulates much about the way Harrods adapts to shifting fashions. First opened in 1894, the Fur department thrived as its products achieved the rank of status symbol. In 1936 a massive fur store was built, capable of holding 25,000 garments secure from dust, water, fire and moths within its 700 square metres/7,500 square feet. At the same time Harrods had purchased a patented fur-cleaning system, and the slogan 'Harrodize your furs' attracted many customers. But what was once a highly profitable business suffered a dramatic decline, and in April 1990 Harrods closed its Fur Salon. The cold storage vault at the store continues to provide a service for its 7,500 customers.

## GIFT BUREAU

G is for Gifts – in particular the Wedding Gift Bureau established in 1953. This was far more than a 'Bride's List' department: it guided customers through the sometimes tricky etiquette of what was and was not acceptable as a nuptial gift. Over the years Harrods has turned the tactful giving of advice on society matters into an art form. Now it has also turned it into a science with the introduction in 1985 of the computerised Gift and Bridal Registry on the second floor. This enables the couple to select their wedding gifts without fear of duplication.

## HAIR AND BEAUTY

H is for the Hair and Beauty Salon. By 1909 Harrods was claiming its Ladies' Hairdressing Courts were 'unquestionably the finest in the world', offering thirty-three richly decorated hairdressing, manicure and chiropody courts set around comfortable lounges. In 1924 it was encouraging customers to try out the latest styles with an offer of 'a charming coiffure for 10 guineas' (7 guineas for front only). Pampering the lady customers obviously paid off, for in 1936 an enormous beauty parlour occupying half an acre was opened. The *Morning Post* described the seventy-two rooms as 'the finest salons in the world dedicated to beauty of face, figure and hair'. It was particularly enthusiastic about the facilities in each booth: 'An ivory telephone is at your right hand awaiting the calls you may wish to make to friends. A tray for tea, writing or reading swings into place on your left.' The atmosphere of luxury bordering on hedonism has been maintained in the modern Hair and Beauty Salon, which in 1982 was moved to the fifth floor. The largest and most luxurious in-store salon in Europe, it covers 1,160 square metres/12,500 square feet and features twenty-five shampoo positions, nineteen beauty rooms and, at its centre, an evergreen tree in a water garden.

Also in 1982 a Children's Hairdressing department was opened adjacent to Children's Wear on the first floor. Its users can have their fringe tidied or the ponytail clipped among decorations from the tales of Beatrix Potter. A barbershop is also available on the ground floor.

## HARRODS SHOP

H is also for Harrods Shop – a department set up in 1982 stocking only merchandise bearing Harrods' famous logo. The idea was an immediate success and branches are now found at the department store Nihombashi in Tokyo, on the Cunard liner *QE2*, on *The Queen Mary*, and at airports at Frankfurt, London Heathrow and Toronto.

Harrods could not only supply everything for the home, it provided houses as well, as shown in this 1921 advertisement.

## HOUSE BUILDING

H is for Houses, too. During the 1920s Harrods was more than happy to build a customer's home for them – an advertisement of the time shows one allegedly in the Tudor style. If ever proof were needed that there is nothing Harrods cannot provide, surely this is it!

## IRONMONGERY

I is for Ironmongery. In 1909 this department was one of the largest in the store, offering a huge range of items. According to the store's own booklet, *The House that Every Woman Knows*, the merchandise included:

Sewing Machines, Lawn Mowers and Rollers, Perambulators, Garden Furniture, Wire Netting, Baths, Knife Cleaners, Mincing Machines, household utensils in Copper, Tin, Aluminium and other metals, Bird

In 1909 the Ironmongery department was divided into two sections:
Artistic and Kitchen Ironmongery.

Cages, Clothes Racks, Coal Vases, Cruets, Dish Covers, Enamel Ware, Fenders and Fireirons, Seat Fenders, Fire Guards and Screens, Gas Fittings, Refrigerators and Ice Safes of all sizes, Table Gongs, Jelly, etc Moulds, Ranges, Spirit Lamps, Stoves, Tool Cabinets, Weighing Machines, Wringing and Mangling Machines, etc.

It seems amazing that the first floor did not give up the struggle under the weight of all that iron!

### ICE CREAM

I is also for the first British in-store Ice Cream Parlour which opened in 1976, specialising in American-style ice cream.

### JEWELLERY

J is for Jewellery. The Jewellery department began as a humble counter with a few inexpensive items on show, but in 1911 Harrods unveiled an extravagantly furnished Gem Room where the showcases had ormolu fittings and the walls were of marble.

The Fine Jewellery Room, opened in 1989, is encased in an opulent neo-Classical setting on the ground floor. It features ranges from seven of the world's finest jewellers plus exhibitions of the latest designs.

### KITCHENWARE

K is for Kitchenware. Always a stalwart at the store, the department came into its own in 1982 with the opening of Cook's Way on the second floor:

2,400 square metres/26,000 square feet of marble malls devoted to everything the modern chef could possibly need, plus mountains of kitchenware and kitchen furniture.

## KENNELS

K is also for Kennels. Harrods welcomed its customers' pets for a hundred years (at first by allowing dogs to be tied to railings outside the store) and the store's basement kennels were thought to be unique among department stores across the globe.

## LIBRARY

L is for Library. Opened on the first day of World War I, this evolved into the largest private circulating library in the world, and in its heyday ninety-seven staff were required to keep track of the 40,000 subscribers. Each librarian dealt with one set of customers, getting to know their likes

The Library early this century. Originally run by a book club,
it was expanded and taken into the Harrods fold in 1914.

and dislikes so well that selections were agreed from a telephone call. Thus it was that Library staff chose the Queen Mother's reading matter twice a week for many years, and were known to deliver a library book a day to Sir Winston Churchill in the 1960s. Eventually it became something of an anachronism, however, taking up a large area, producing insignificant profits, and in effect competing with the Books department. With its subscribers reduced to a faithful band of 1,100, the Harrods Library was finally shut down in August 1989.

## LINENS

L is also for the Linen department, which at one time held renowned 'White Sales' when its goods were sculpted into lions, bears and friezes.

Serried ranks of canes in the Man's Shop of 1930. The department had
something of the atmosphere of a men's club.

## MENSWEAR

M was once for Millinery, a stalwart among Harrods departments for
many years. But now that this old-fashioned term has disappeared (and
with it a huge space devoted to allowing genteel ladies to try on hats at their
leisure), the letter stands for Menswear. Harrods' development along Hans
Crescent in late Victorian times created the opportunity to open a man's
shop. By the early 1900s it was offering anything from personally tailored
military or dress uniforms, with matching sword, to motor car clothing.

Harrods provided club rooms and smoking rooms stylish enough to
rival any West End club. In 1919 the store was able to boast that 'the
Ready-to-Wear section is rapidly becoming most popular with busy men
averse to the tedium and inconvenience of waiting while their clothes are
made to measure'. In the late 1920s the Man's Shop was expanded, with
greater emphasis on space, elegance and comfort. Beautifully carved
wooden display tables replaced the glass cases, and the area looked more
like a drawing room than a sales floor.

The menswear staff aped their female colleagues in 1948 when the first
Harrods fashion show for men was held, heralded by a bugler. It was
something of an oddity for its time but succeeded in making a barbed point
at its close, for in strolled the department controller decked out in an open
shirt, knotted handkerchief, and red braces to support his rolled-up
trousers. The spectacle was designed to amuse but also to shame male
customers into adopting more stylish garb. Today men at Harrods can
choose from 500 different types of shirts, and 9,000 ties to go with them. A
large department known as Leisure Man opened in 1977, and in 1990

Harrods commenced a major renovation of the Man's Shop, to re-create the elegance and sophistication of Harrods' menswear in the 1930s.

## MOTOR CARS

M is also for Motor Cars, which Harrods began selling in 1902. A company advertisement included details of the 10 horsepower 'Progress' Tonneau at £365. Eighty years on, it was offering a special Range Rover Car decorated in the green and gold Harrods livery.

## MAIL ORDER

M is for Mail Order, too. This has long been a Harrods service but was extended in 1967 with the introduction of the Harrods Home Shopping Service, a new scheme to sell children's wear by post.

## NEEDLEWORK

N is for Needlework, an early and major attraction at the store. Known as the Art Needlework department, it is still going strong today.

## NURSERY

N is also for a less enduring idea. In 1921 *Harrods News* invited visitors to 'leave your tots in the Harrods nursery'. The efforts of frazzled assistants trying to keep youngsters entertained while their parents loitered through the store took their toll (insurance problems would have been another factor in killing the idea) and the nursery was quickly and quietly dropped.

## OLYMPIC WAY

O is for the Olympic Way, the comprehensive sports complex introduced in 1977. Initially, it occupied 2,000 square metres/half an acre on the fourth floor. However, such was its success in promoting the latest in equipment and clothing for sport that it was transplanted in expanded form to the fifth floor at the end of 1990 – the first time the fifth floor has been used seriously as selling space, and renamed the Sports and Leisure Complex.

## PIANOS

P is for the Piano department. No self-respecting middle-class home of the early twentieth century was without a piano, and Harrods was one of the biggest stockists in the country. An enlarged Piano and Gramophone department was opened in 1925. The department had a team of tuners who travelled the country maintaining the tunefulness of Harrods pianos. In 1952 there were 20,000 contracts, being serviced by a team of thirty. One tuner turned up at a large house in Cumberland to be met with the question, 'Have you brought the fish? I sent a telegram to the store today asking them to send some halibut up with you for my dinner party this evening.' The tuner had to confess he had not travelled especially from

Knightsbridge to see to her piano and deliver a few groceries. Today the department offers 150 pianos for sale – still impressive, but markedly down on the 700 it once used to stock.

A real novelty in 1955 was the Personal Recording Service available from a soundproofed room tucked behind the pianos. Here customers could record their own message on to 12.5 cm/5 inch vinyl discs. The idea proved particularly popular for Christmas messages, and countless unique missives were recorded in the studio.

Perfumes spell luxury and elegance – and so are perfectly suited to Harrods!
This fantastic array of carefully positioned little bottles was photographed around 1914.

## PERFUMES HALL

P is also for the Perfumes Hall in the middle of the ground floor, which is believed to carry the finest and most exotic selection of perfumes in the world on its 557 square metres/6,000 square feet. Built in 1985, the hall is faced in Norwegian charcoal granite complemented by steel, mirrors, and hand-sculptured glass. It is as magnificent as its early predecessor in 1919, which was similarly luxurious and kept its fragrant aromas to itself behind enormous mahogany doors.

## PORTRAIT STUDIO

In addition, P is for the Harrods Portrait Studio, where customers had their pictures taken throughout this century. During the London Season, the arrangement was that 'Ladies and Gentlemen attending Courts and Levées may have special sittings at any hour of the day or night'. In 1929 the department was offering a special deal, when for three guineas it would photograph children annually from their first to their twenty-first birthday – evidence of continuity of custom, if nothing else!

## QUERIES

Q is for Queries. With 35,000 customers visiting this large and complex store every day, questions ranging from 'Where are the toilets?' to 'How do I get to the Insurance department?' are inevitable. Such was the volume of foreign visitors by 1968 that the store took on a team of interpreters to help handle their enquiries. Patient assistants man information desks around the store, which also provides department lists in seven languages and has a special interpreters' desk for Japanese visitors.

## QUALITY

Q is also, of course, for Quality. It is its reputation for quality which Harrods has always prided itself on most of all.

Quality is often so intangible that it cannot be measured, but in 1924 Harrods set up a quality-control laboratory for testing textiles. The first department of its kind in a retail store, it was located on the fifth floor and checked the standard of all textiles that were sold at Harrods, using a device known as a 'Fadeometer' to assess how the fabrics coped with long exposure to light.

In 1963 the department was instrumental in helping Harrods to pioneer the introduction of cleaning instruction labels on clothes with its 'Fashion Fabric Care Scheme'. Ahead of the rest of the textiles industry, Harrods began stitching washing and fabric care instructions into the appropriate merchandise, a move applauded at the time as a major step forward in helping the customer maintain goods at their best.

In 1968 the textiles laboratory was still going strong, investigating 2,700 product complaints a year for the Harrods Group. But the closure of the Harrods workrooms and the contracting out of the manufacture of own-label goods led to the department's demise in the 1970s.

## RESTAURANTS

R is for Restaurants. Harrods has been providing customers with an opportunity to pause for refreshment since 1891, with a ground floor restaurant opening three years later, followed by the huge Grand Restaurant in 1900. From 1911 tea could be enjoyed in the Rock Tea Gardens on the roof of the building.

Today the store features eleven restaurants, from the West Side Express on the ground floor to the 500-seat Georgian Restaurant on the fourth, where the Terrace cocktail bar can also be found. Also worthy of note is the health juice bar. Introduced in 1954 after a manager returned from Switzerland inspired by the idea of serving pure fruit and vegetable drinks, the bar has seen its popularity rise with the health trend.

Harrods even has its own pub, The Green Man. Decked out in Jacobean style, it is the first public house to be built in a department store – quite an irony in view of the trouble Sir Richard Burbidge took to get rid of The Buttercup public house which was cluttering up his site!

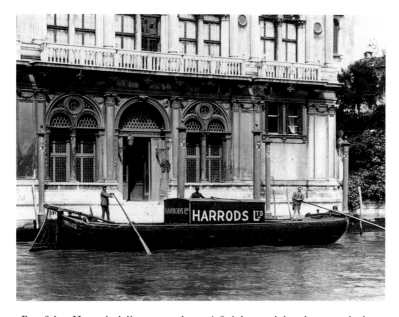

Proof that Harrods delivers anywhere. A freight gondola takes over the last stage of a furniture delivery to Venice in 1929.

## REMOVALS

R is also for Removals. Harrods' removals service had ferried furniture for many top people in its time – it has been said that 'people vote out governments but Harrods moves in Prime Ministers'.

The service was worldwide. In one instance, a Harrods van floated the final few miles of a delivery to Venice in a gondola. For another job, in 1963, the department spent fifty-three days transporting furniture and effects to the new Persian Hilton.

## SHOES

S is for Shoes. In 1909 the store described its Ladies' Boot and Shoe department as 'a veritable Palace of Footwear filled with dainty and elegant shapes and styles and every convenience for ladies to make selections'. Twenty years later, children's shoes had been added to the stock. An assistant recalled that there was 'a fine set of unique chairs for children, mounted on carefully designed platforms of Ancona walnut. These model revolving armchairs are very fascinating from the youngster's

The Ladies' Boot and Shoe department in Edwardian times.
The stated aim was 'to fit every foot to perfection'.

point of view, and are instrumental in soothing the restless child who prefers to romp rather than try on shoes, and leaves him with a desire to visit Harrods again.' How much the assistant relished welcoming back the little rascals who insisted on constantly swinging round on the chairs is another matter...

The spirit of Harrods' service is equally apparent in another incident, this time from 1937. A man found a left shoe lying in the street and, noticing it had a Harrods label, contacted the store. Equipped with the shoe number and size, staff traced the date it had been bought and, from those records, the customer's name. Thus it was that a man in Cirencester was astounded to receive a parcel from Harrods containing the left shoe that had fallen from his car in London a few days before.

## TOYS

T is for Toys. Countless children have made their first visit to the famous emporium in order to visit its magnificent Toy department, their eyes widening at the massive and beautifully constructed displays. *The Sphere* of 1922 commented, 'The Toyland Section of Harrods great store at this season of the year is one of the sights of London, and perhaps of any of the civilised capitals of the world.' The sentiment is just as true today, as any visitor to the fourth floor can confirm.

## TRAVEL AND TICKETS

T is also for Travel and Tickets. Harrods has had its own Travel and Tickets Agency from 1897. Taking nearly £4,000 that year, it proved more of a money-spinner than departments such as Millinery. The service bears out the Harrods claim to be able to offer everything needed in life under one roof – after you book your holiday, off you go to purchase the necessary clothes and a trunk to put them in. Or if you are just going to the theatre, you can buy the tickets from Harrods, then hire your evening wear and a car to take you on to supper afterwards. Today the Travel Bureau and Theatre Tickets agency are housed on the lower ground floor.

## UNDERTAKING

U is for Undertaking. True to its claim to be able to supply customers with everything they need from cradle to grave, Harrods had its own funerals service. It was already well-established in 1900 and was only recently dropped from the list of services offered.

## UNIFORMS

U is also for Uniforms of all kinds – from those for the services to the many different uniforms worn at the schools to which Harrods customers send their children. The shop is not known as 'the Eton of stores' for nothing.

## VAULT

V is for Vault. The Harrods Safe Deposit was launched in a blaze of publicity in 1896, a massive array of elaborately decorated strongrooms set beneath the store. The vault was purchased in Glasgow by Woodman Burbidge on one of his first buying trips, and he negotiated a competitive price, much to the pride of his father the managing director. It has hardly changed from that time to this.

Customers are required to give their own password to gain entry, and on occasions staff have been required to gently prompt forgetful customers by discreetly murmuring childhood jingles or popular songs. An incident from 1954 has been repeated in different ways over the decades: Lord Ulick Browne came to collect some documents he had deposited ten years before. He could not recall the password he had scribbled on a piece of paper and handed in at the time. 'Something to do with entertainment,' prompted the attendant. 'Theatre?' guessed his Lordship. 'Wrong, it begins with J,' replied the guard. 'Jazz?' 'Getting warmer, try something connected with dancing.' After drawing a blank with 'jitterbug' Lord Ulick struck lucky with 'jive', enabling the Harrods man to let him in with a 'pass, friend'.

The Safe Deposit has attracted its share of eccentrics, too. One regular user of the 1950s used to enter his vault with an empty pipe, and emerge with it filled with tobacco. Eventually he committed suicide and when his box was opened, sure enough, it held only a pouch of tobacco.

Safe Deposit

At Harrods even the Safe Deposit vault is elegant! Purchased in 1896 by Woodman Burbidge, it is very little changed today.

## WAY IN

W is for Way In, the department offering young fashions to the Harrods regulars of the future. The idea was conceived in the mid 1960s, when the average age of Harrods customers was rising and the store seemed anti-quated in comparison with the trendy boutiques in Carnaby Street and the Kings Road. Way In began as a separate company, owned by Harrods, trading on the fourth floor with separate access and different opening hours to the rest of the shop. The decor was dark with spotlights pinpointing different sections among the nineteen departments. Among these were a juice bar, blow-up photographs service, records, accessories and fashion clothing, including the new unisex styles.

For a traditional department store such as Harrods it was a daring step. It worked: Way In was one of the top boutiques in London for about eight years, setting trends in fashion, trading hours and display techniques and attracting many stars of the day. Its constantly evolving range of co-ordinated, colour-matched clothes took the fashion world by storm. The 100 or so staff were recruited through a series of learning sessions at hotels, and were chosen for their affinity with boutiques rather than with the top people's store. Women were decked out in mini dresses, and men in brown jumpers, the initial experiments with white jackets and black flared trousers being deemed a failure. The setting of daily sales targets resulted in something of a crush of sales assistants round the till to claim the com-missions on purchases by customers who had wandered in and made their choice without the benefit of advice. Way In even sponsored a boat, the *Psychedelic Surfer*, in the Round Britain Power Boat Race of 1968. But shoplifting was a major problem in the murky decor, and the fickle young fashion market changed its allegiances. It was the end of an era. In 1974 Way In was revamped. Ten years later it was totally redesigned in a £3 million transformation that included a new interior and the introduction of the Way In cosmetics range.

## WINE

W is also for Wine. Harrods has long been famous for its selection of wine and still has extensive cellars underneath the building. Earlier this century, half of all the wine Harrods sold was bottled on the premises – no mean feat considering the total sales of 176,000 litres/38, 692 gallons in 1934! In 1972 the Wine department was rebuilt as a Spanish bodega with an even larger range of wines and spirits, including more than 160 whiskies.

## X-RAY (AND THE HIRE DEPARTMENT)

X is always for X-Ray, of course, but its application here is only slightly far-fetched, because during the heyday of Harrods Motor Hire the department was able to offer a well-equipped ambulance complete with trained nurse (but not, admittedly, any X-ray apparatus).

Harrods began providing motor vehicles for hire in 1907. It is thought to be the oldest such service in the world. Private cars with chauffeurs came with the assurance that 'should any mishap befall either the Chauffeur or the Car, Harrods will effect immediate replacement'.

The hire service was extended to include boats of all kinds, which could be launched on the stretch of the Thames owned by Harrods near the Barnes depository. Hearses and, from 1935, four aircraft were also available for hire. At the peak of its popularity in 1933, the service allowed clients use of a chauffeured Armstrong Siddeley, day and night for the year, at a set price of £180. The publicity slogan was 'The car is yours. The care is ours,' and it proved so popular that a fleet of 110 cars was needed in order to keep up with demand.

The Harrods ambulance in 1930. It was available for hire, complete with nurse.

Harrods met many of its customers' needs through the Hire department – early this century *Harrods News* was able to offer entertainers for parties such as 'Edgar B Skeet for Dramatic and Humorous Recitals, Musical Sketches, & c, from £4.0'. Mr Skeet's services were available within a six-kilometre/four-mile radius of the store.

## YOUNG DESIGNERS

Y is for the Young Designers Room on the first floor, which housed work by leading young designers and filled the gap between well-established designers and the new directional ones to be found in Way In. Its opening in 1985 was further evidence of the deliberate shift towards young contemporary fashion which Harrods has taken.

The Young Designers Room was an example of Harrods' policy
of catering for all age groups.

## ZOO

Z is for Zoo, the popular name for the store's Pet Shop department, which was once one of its most famous sections. Many is the child who has been bribed through enduring a long shopping trip with the promise of a visit to the 'Harrods Zoo'. It began by offering live poultry from 1917, and was known as the Livestock department for some years before it progressed to offering animals as pets rather than food.

Veronica the tapir became a Harrods legend. Admiring the beast is
Dame Margot Fonteyn, photographed in 1968.

Children were particularly attracted to the forty different kinds of
exotic birds usually on show. Most of the department's turnover was in
pedigree dogs, but it promised to supply any animal in the world. At one
time the department's chief attraction was a tapir called Veronica, a
sociable beast who would follow the keepers as they cleaned out the cages,
vacuuming up any leftovers with her snout. She was prone to bolting into
the adjacent Carpets department on occasion, much to the consternation of
its customers.

Escapes from the Pet Shop are the stuff of legend at the store: several
squirrels got out and were not returned until they had been cornered in the
cellars several months later. Snakes were banished from the section after
one surprised a salesgirl opening a drawer of baby clothes. One monkey
found a different way to misbehave: it snatched an average of three pairs of
spectacles a day from customers who ventured too near its cage, and once
whipped off a man's wig. The animal tried the toupé on, scrunched it up in
disgust, and thrust it back through the bars to its owner, who bundled it
into his pocket and marched off.

The department was famous throughout the world, and senior staff
appeared on television programmes in the 1960s giving advice on buying
and keeping animals. Stricter regulations on the sale of wild animals
severely curtailed trade in the 1970s, but the department survives today,
providing yet another example of the remarkable range of goods and
services Harrods has offered throughout its life.

# PRESENTS FOR THE TROOPS
# IN SOUTH AFRICA.

## WAR OFFICE LIST OF ARTICLES REQUIRED.

The following official list of articles required by the Troops in South Africa has been prepared from the best information available at the War Office, but it does not pretend to be exhaustive, and is published only as a suggestion:

*Tobacco, *Cigars, *Cigarettes, Briar Pipes, small Lanterns and Candles, Sweets, Jam, &c., Pocket Knives, portable Mincing Machines, *Knitted Socks (good quality only), *Worsted Nightcaps or Tam-o'-Shanters, Cardigan Waistcoats, Flannel Shirts, Woollen Drawers and Vests, Cholera Belts, Slippers or Canvas Shoes, Shoe Laces, Neck Mufflers, Pocket Handkerchiefs, Writing Materials, i.e., Letter Books, containing Sheets of Paper, an Ink Pencil, and Envelopes.

The articles marked with an asterisk are believed to be most in demand.  Parcels containing matches of any kind cannot be received.

# HARRODS STORES, Ltd.

Having been granted facilities by H.M. Customs and the War Office, will supply any of the above goods, specially packed for Export to South Africa, and the same will be delivered

## Duty and  Carriage Free

to any Member of our Forces in distribution, to the General Officer

South Africa (or, if for ordinary commanding Lines of communication).

*OMNIA OMNIBUS UBIQUE*

Special Quotations appended for List of Goods recommended for the purpose.

## LAMBERT & BUTLER'S Log Cabin, Navy Cut, or Richmond Mixture.

Packed in ¼-lb., ½-lb., or 1-lb. Tins.

AT **2/3** PER LB., OR **5** lbs. FOR **11/-**

(Ordinary price in England 5/6 to 6/- per lb.)

## A ¼ lb. Tin of Tobacco with Briar Pipe IN BOX COMPLETE, 1/-

VIKING NAVY CUT CIGARETTES at 1s. 3d. per 100 (in Tins of 50),
CIGARETTE HOLDER INCLUDED.

Special Quotations for Cigars and other Brands of Cigarettes in quantities on Application.

All Tobacco specially packed in hermetically sealed tins to keep any length of time in any climate.

LIST CONTINUED ON OTHER SIDE

A record of Harrods' support for British forces during the Boer War
(1899–1902).

# CHAPTER SEVEN

# TRYING TIMES

*Harrods*

# "A factor in the National life"

An enterprise of Harrods' size is a microcosm of the nation. A deeply patriotic store with a strong sense of responsibility, it has made great efforts to support Britain at times of strife and, particularly, times of war. This nationalism is perhaps fostered in part by the store's close relationship with the Royal Family, and also the fact that Harrods is virtually a national institution. However, retailing also has quite a lot in common with military life, for they share the characteristics of strong discipline, excellent organisation and a rigid management structure. Perhaps this also helps to explain the affinity Harrods has felt with the armed forces for many years, which it has shown in its support for their activities. The store's proximity to a barracks and the regular custom it enjoys from Chelsea Pensioners may have added to Harrods' resolve.

## EQUIPPING THE CIV FORCE DURING THE BOER WAR

The first time Harrods supported British forces was in 1899 during the Boer War in South Africa. Harrods chairman Alfred Newton was also Lord Mayor of London that year, and he launched an appeal for raising and equipping the City Imperial Volunteers (CIV) force. Given his position within Harrods, very little persuasion was required before the store provided massive support with items such as helmets, saddles, mules and provisions, sufficient for it to claim to have equipped the CIV almost single-handedly. This level of assistance was sustained throughout the war, and when the triumphant CIV force returned in October 1900 Harrods sent a large convoy to meet the men at Southampton and present them with 1,250 luncheon packages.

An inspection of the Territorial Army at Harrods in 1909. The store
supported the Territorials and provided incentives for staff to join this
reserve force.

### INCENTIVES TO JOIN THE TERRITORIALS

Harrods encouraged its staff to join the Territorials, the Army's reserve
force from this time, and indeed from 1905 allowed recruits an extra week's
holiday for the necessary annual training. Later, the privileges for
employees who joined the Territorials included a bonus for completing
training, payment of regimental subscriptions, and cycles available at cost
price to help them travel to Territorial activities.

### OUTBREAK OF WORLD WAR I

On 7 September 1914 managing director Richard Burbidge used a full
page of the staff newspaper, the *Harrodian Gazette*, to say, 'I think it is the
duty of all men between the ages of 19 and 35 strongly to support Lord
Kitchener's appeal for recruits for the Army.' He promised a £2 bonus to
every Harrods man who enlisted, and announced that the store would
consider granting half salary to their mothers if they were dependent
widows. The hunt was on for men to fight in World War I, and the effects
on life at the store were dramatic.

Departments competed to boast the highest proportion of staff who
had signed up, and the staff newspaper carried many snide comments and
cartoons deriding able-bodied men who refused to fight for their country.

By 1916 2,000 men from Harrods were in the services, and the family support for their wives, mothers and children was costing the firm £6,000 a year. Looking at the figures of payments to dependants, it is clear that the majority of staff who went to war were single. For example, of the 639 members of staff who had enlisted by November 1914, only 168 wives or mothers were receiving half pay. The *Harrodian Gazette* questioned the motives of some couples tying the knot: 'Is it true,' it wondered, 'that the unmarried members of our Staff who are also members of His Majesty's Forces are contemplating embarking on the voyage of matrimony in order to qualify for half-pay while on service? Girls, mark your man!'

The girls were doing more than marking their men: they were replacing them. Until now women had formed a minority of staff, but from this time the sexes were represented equally on the Harrods payroll. Even

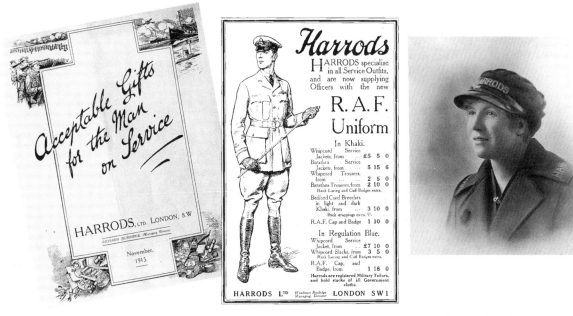

LEFT AND CENTRE: Harrods had everything for the men in the services, as these leaflets illustrate. RIGHT: Women were drafted in to replace the men in the store in wartime. Shown here is Dorothy Adams, aged 21, who joined the Harrods despatch team during World War I.

the Green Men, the tall, green-uniformed commissionaires who manned the store's entrances, were replaced by Green Women for a while. The wider acceptance of the idea of women taking employment changed the perception of the female sex throughout society.

### LETTERS FROM STAFF AT THE FRONT

The *Harrodian Gazette* carried innumerable letters from the Front, their early excitement in battle and optimism about the War waning poignantly into a yearning for it to end and for an early return home. The letters from staff vividly evoke the blend of boredom and excitement typical of life at the Front. The messages of goodwill in the newspapers from this era reveal strong bonds between staff of the same department – the 'Harrods family' was probably more real at this time than ever, through the links forged within departments by the common bond of war.

Staff reported chance meetings with each other on foreign soil, and they occasionally recognised customers too. Gunner Green tells such a story: 'The other day my captain came up to me and said "Do you remember serving me with this pair of shoes, Green?" Knowing him quite well from the old store I said "yes sir, and if you look inside you will find the number and size, 6930, 9 1/2, fitting E."' As a result, Green commented with some satisfaction, he ended up spending less time on guard duty, and more on the task of cleaning the Captain's shoes!

A number of Harrods staff put their driving or stock management skills to good use in the services. Private W Wright wrote from the Mechanical Transport Department in St Albans that 'being a mechanic, and my services to His Majesty being confined to travelling on the steam lorries which carry the supplies to the troops in St Albans and round about, I get no route-marching, no sore feet, and only a minimum of drill and exercise.' Private Wright went on to say that he had consequently put on seven pounds in a month.

### SUPPORTING THE WAR EFFORT

Harrods issued regular food parcels to its staff at the Front. These provided entertainment as well as comfort, according to one letter from a sergeant thanking staff for their presents of chocolate, cigarettes, tobacco and handkerchiefs. He described how the prized package 'was kept for about half an hour before it was opened, as when a parcel arrives everybody has to guess the contents and, when it is opened, all those who are right have a share of it. This causes great fun.' Harrods also provided hampers of tea, cake, biscuits, sugar and butter to wives and dependent widowed mothers – evidence of its strong belief that it had a responsibility to aid all who were part of 'The House of Harrod'.

The store sold hampers for despatch to the front, as well as uniforms (including the Harrods service boot) and other items for use by the services. *The Sphere* reports on one such product: 'At Messrs Harrods one is always sure to find the very latest novelties... An extremely inexpensive, though very valuable gift for any man on active service is a small but effective pocket periscope which will serve him also as a shaving mirror.' The store also sold compasses with measure markings so that those at home could follow the progress of the War on a map.

For those who liked to play at war, the Harrods rifle range on the roof of the Trevor Square building was proving a great success and was transferred to a larger space on the fifth floor of the main store. It was

Harrods staff rallied to help those fighting abroad during both World Wars, knitting comforts, preparing food parcels and raising funds. Here they are finishing off extra clothing to be sent to troops in 1941.

believed to encourage men to sign up, but in the main it became a spot for customers to try out the killing equipment without risk to themselves.

Harrods provided far more practical help at this time by sending staff from its building department out to Belgium and northern France to convert hotels into hospitals and to construct aeroplane sheds. In one such project a building at La Panne was converted and expanded into a 640-bed hospital. Mr Herbert Costa, manager of the Harrods building and electrical departments, was later presented with the Order and Symbol of l'Ordre Leopold II by the King of Belgium in recognition of his considerable efforts in that country.

### RATIONS . . . AND RECOMPENSE

Back in London, deliveries were restricted by the darkness of the streets as lighting economies were introduced, and many of the horses Harrods had purchased to make its deliveries were given to the army. Such was the fear of fire that any staff found carrying matches would be immediately dismissed.

Scrimping and saving became a national pastime, and Harrods set up its own Food Bureau on 30 August 1917. Acting in advance of government instructions, it introduced rationing of certain goods for all customers. Sugar, for example, was restricted to 340 grams/12 ounces per head a week, and Harrods soon had 42,928 registered customers for sugar alone. Within weeks the Food Bureau had answered 250,000 enquiries about economical cookery, and backed up its advice with lectures, demonstrations and recipe cards. Such were the shortages that patient shoppers were forced to queue at the store for their rationed chocolate – an event unheard of before then at the top people's store.

At the close of the War, which claimed the lives of 147 Harrodians, Woodman Burbidge issued a letter to staff.

Dear Co-Worker,

In this hour of Victory it is indeed a special pleasure to express the gratitude of the Directors, and my own personal gratitude, firstly to all those men of Harrods who have rendered such splendid service to their Country in the War, and secondly to every one of you who has so loyally helped us here. We fully recognise such services to be beyond the usual means of recompense, but they are not beyond appreciation, and as a token of our appreciation it has been decided –

1. To utilize a Fund of £10,000 to ease the anxieties of men of Harrods broken in battle and to provide them with a measure of help along the road.

2. To set aside a grant of up to £5,000 for necessitous cases among those Harrods warriors who are able to resume their work.

3. To grant every member of our staff with an additional week's pay, and to those who were with us on 4 August 1914, and who are still in our employ, with two weeks' pay.

The letter surprised his fellow directors, for they had not been consulted. Nevertheless, Harrods continued to show its gratitude to those who had fought in the war. For example, the store provided twenty lorries to transport 8,000 men wounded in the conflict to an entertainment at the Wigmore Hall in March 1923.

## THE GENERAL STRIKE

The General Strike of 1926 faced Harrods with a different kind of problem. No store which prides itself on its service is prepared to close, but the logistics of transporting its (loyal and non-unionised) staff in to man the tills and keep the stock flowing were daunting. Fortunately the company had a ready-made fleet of buses to carry its workers – the despatch vans. The store's basement was converted into a bus station for staff, but once they emerged the buses occasionally ran the gauntlet of stone-throwers near the bus depots, and had to call on the store's own special constabulary for protection from the strikers.

The Harrodian section of the Metropolitan Special Constabulary had been founded more than a decade before. (There is an account of a contingent in 1911 parading equipped with pith helmets, armlets and whistles, with chair legs for truncheons.) They were paid a small fee to be available for policing duties in addition to their normal jobs, but were called into street service in 1926 – and many were pelted with eggs for their trouble. Harrods, in fact, formed the largest individual section of all such constabularies in the city, numbering 150 members by 1939. By that time Harrods had also set up its own Territorial Army Unit, part of the 27th battalion of the Territorials.

## THE STORE DURING WORLD WAR II

All such resources were called on with the onset of World War II in August 1939. A ton and a half of cardboard was used to block up the store's windows, and 18,000 sandbags were filled by staff. They were now required to carry gas masks with them at all times because of the fear of mustard gas attack, which never in fact occurred. Sir Woodman told staff, 'I say to you now what I said to the staff in the last War, and that is "Keep the flag flying. It is patriotic, it applies to your work, and it applies to Harrods" and do as much National Service as possible.' By now Miss Stacey of the Fur department was organising a party to knit comforts for the troops in France, and soon staff had set up their own Comforts Fund, to ensure a supply of goods such as cigarettes to the troops.

On 6 December 1939, Sir Woodman led an inspection of the Air Raid Protection staff (ARP) at Harrods. The party viewed the first aid facilities in the Banking Hall, and then prepared to continue its tour via the recently

An inspection of Harrods' ARP (Air Raid Protection staff) at the store
by Sir Philip Garne in 1940.

installed escalators by Door 5. Here the enthusiastic ARP staff had arranged to show their readiness for action with a fake explosion. They let rip, bashing iron sheets, rattling metal dustbins, flashing arc lamps, and generally simulating the noise and havoc of a bomb attack. Unfortunately, the touring party was not as well-prepared, and an unseemly gallop back to the safety of the Banking Hall rather detracted from the impact of the demonstration.

Nine months later the store suffered its first bomb strike, but in fact the premises survived virtually unscathed from the War, apart from the Estates Office, which was completely destroyed by a doodlebug in 1944. Harrods was well-equipped for such conditions: self-sufficient in water and electricity, and concealing large underground spacers beneath its sturdily constructed exterior.

There are 1,880 names in the books recording war service by Harrods staff. Although this figure is less than in the previous war, the store, like the country, was hit harder. Sparsely lit, it was open only from 10am to 4pm and offered a restricted delivery service (the despatch radius was halved to thirty-two kilometres/twenty miles). Yet it maintained its tradition of topical displays, with exhibitions of life in Greece, Jugoslavia, Czechoslovakia, Poland and other Allied nations, featuring tableaux of conditions in peace and war, and collections to raise funds for aid.

## SUPPLYING THE TROOPS

The clothing workrooms began making uniforms, while aircraft parts and parachutes were produced in the Harrods factories. Harrods vans were requisitioned for army use – causing some soldiers in Africa to do a double

From military tailoring to stout
shoes, Harrods provided everything
required by service men and women.

take as a Harrods van, still sporting its livery, trundled past them. To some, such sights must have provided a piquant memory of home. In the officers' mess, a Harrods label was regarded as the mark of a gentleman. One customer wrote to the store:

> My son's RAF uniform has given entire satisfaction. I would like to point out that Messrs Harrods have attired my son since birth. Such matters are of small account these days but it is interesting to recall that first of all his baby clothes were supplied by Messrs Harrods Baby Linen Department, then the Little Boy's Department provided what was necessary. Later on schooldays when the Boy's outfitting dressed him for Rugby and afterwards Cambridge, and now the Man's Shop have turned him out very smartly for the RAF.

### LIFE DURING THE WAR

The promotional newsletter *Harrods News* was reduced in size, and in 1941 it announced, with typically genteel phrasing, 'With the publication of this Christmas number we much regret that by Government order Harrods News must, for the time being, go into retirement.' The following June the National Savings Movement wrote to Sir Woodman congratulating him on his announcement that there would be no July Sale, to discourage unnecessary spending. The restaurant also set a maximum price of 5/- per meal for the same reasons. A more effective bar on spending was provided by petrol and train shortages. These inhibited shopping trips into town for the many regular customers who had retreated to the country or even abroad for the duration of the War.

During World War II a Food Advice Service was
organised at Harrods, dispensing advice
on nutrition and economy tips.

By this time the Royal Navy and the Canadian Air Force were occupying parts of the building – which was in part infested with rats as maintenance went neglected – and the basement was converted into an air raid shelter. Times were hard, but people still snatched what entertainment they could to cheer up the daily grind. The ARP apparently held some particularly memorable parties in the Georgian Restaurant and later the basement cafe.

In 1943 Marguerite Patten (later famous as a television broadcaster and cookery writer) joined Harrods to run its Food Advice Service, dispensing suggestions on how to cook within the limitations imposed by rationing. (Typical weekly allowances were 50 grammes/2 ounces butter and 225 grammes/8 ounces sugar; eggs were usually only available in dried

Marguerite Patten ran the demonstrations in the Food Halls during
World War II and eventually became a broadcaster.

form.) She found many of the Harrods customers attending her twice-daily demonstrations in the Meat Hall had a particular problem: 'Many of them had never even cooked before – they had servants to do it for them.' Showing a dowager the basics of cooking lent an egalitarian air to the proceedings, and Marguerite Patten recalls the atmosphere at the store as one of 'incredible matiness – if people could help you, they would, with advice, spare rations or just by listening.'

The bureau eventually closed in 1952, as did the home appliance version on the second floor. Marguerite Patten and her team did a great deal to help customers cope with shortages in the home, for the post-war years were a harsh contrast to the boom that followed World War I.

## VICTORY CELEBRATIONS

Early in May 1945 the War finally ended and the nation rejoiced on VE Day. A massive two-ton 'V for victory' sign was assembled from scrap metal

Harrods was decked out with a two-ton 'V for Victory' sign to celebrate the
ending of hostilities in 1945.

and bolted on to the front of the store, and a huge queue of customers eager to buy something as a mark of celebration stretched down Hans Crescent and round the corner to Basil Street. Only the Food Halls and the Bank were open by this time, and much of the store was in darkness, but this did not diminish the high spirits. When the store closed at 1pm, the excited crowd had to be forced out to continue rejoicing in the streets, and the staff joined in the jubilation.

On 16 May 1945 Sir Richard Burbidge, in a letter to the Harrodian troops, echoed the tone his father Sir Woodman had set at the close of World War I:

> I understand that about half our Forces members will return to us
> during the next twelve months. If you are one of them you will
> find a welcome awaiting you; if you are to stay on for a further
> period in the Forces we wish you good fortune and will see that your
> interests here do not suffer; the bonus [of four weeks' wages] will be
> waiting for you whenever you come back, and your chances of
> progress here will not be affected.

Sir Richard was ready to interview each of these staff as they returned to civilian employment. Apart from his professional attitude towards relations with personnel (he was famous for never forgetting a name), the gesture had links with his own experience. He had risen to the rank of captain in his service during World War I, and he knew how difficult it was to adjust to 'normal' life again.

## INDOMITABLE SPIRIT

It was another thirty years before the normal life of the store was disrupted again, this time as a result of the rise of the international terrorist. Harrods' standing as a national institution, part of the Establishment, marked it out as a target for two bomb attacks in a decade.

Both took place on the last Saturday before Christmas, when the store was brimming with customers on one of the busiest days of the year. On 21 December 1974 a member of staff spotted a suspicious-looking package in the Garden Tools department. She alerted security staff, who realised that the small holdall contained a bomb. They evacuated the area, winding down the fire doors as they left. At 5pm an explosion ripped through the department, but the alertness and efficiency of the staff had prevented any injury. Many volunteers gave up their Sunday rest to come in and help clear up the mess.

Nine years later, on 17 December 1983, the Irish Republican Army planted explosives in a car outside the store in Hans Crescent – where thousands of customers would have gathered had the store been evacuated, which fortunately it was not. Nevertheless, the blast killed six people and injured ninety-three more. The victims of the outrage were supported by a

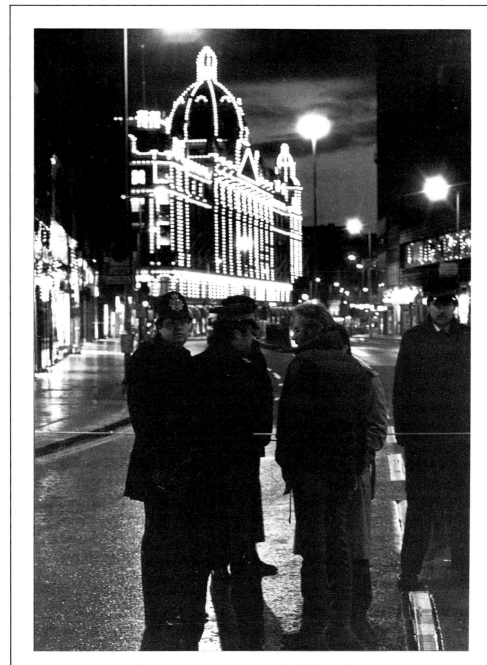

The sad scene on the night of the 1983 bombing.

trust fund set up by the store, and staff showed their loyalty by arriving in their hundreds on their Sunday off to get the store into shape for business the next day.

Tragic though these events are, they highlight the strong spirit of the Harrods staff, and the patriotism the store has shown throughout its life.

Harrods runs a number of special promotions
throughout the year, but for children the Christmas
Toy Fair is the major event at the store.

# CHAPTER EIGHT

# HIGHLIGHTS OF THE YEAR

*Harrods*

# "A veritable Aladdin's Cave"

Fame does not in itself guarantee regular custom for a store; it needs to promote itself energetically too. For more than a century Harrods has demonstrated a flair for self-promotion, ever since Charles Digby Harrod shocked the retail trade with his full-page advertisements.

## THE CHRISTMAS TOY FAIR

The Christmas Toy Fair has invariably been a spectacular extravaganza of exhibitions and toys, presided over by Father Christmas and, originally, the Harrods Fairy. Hundreds of thousands of children have visited Santa in his grotto at the famous store convinced that this was the real thing. Grown-ups flock to Harrods at this time of year too, for they can be sure of finding suitable gifts for all on their list, as well as something to wrap them up in. During the festive season Harrods sells about 148 km/92 miles of ribbon and 28 km/17½ miles of tinsel, a million Christmas cards and a considerable tonnage of mince pies and Christmas puddings.

## IN-STORE EXHIBITIONS

Over the years Harrods has also built a tradition of in-store exhibitions that have been well supported by customers, both old and new.

Being largely autonomous, individual departments have built up their own expertise in special events. One of the most famous of these promotions was held from 22 October to 10 November 1934 in the second-floor China Salon. Harrods had commissioned specimens of work by twenty-seven British artists including Paul Nash, Barbara Hepworth, Graham Sutherland and Clarice Cliff. All were given free rein to design in ceramics, even though many had never worked with such materials before. The Harrods China, Pottery and Glass Exhibition, subtitled 'Modern Art for the Table' was an extraordinary experiment which gripped the public imagination. Demand was astronomical for the limited editions produced of each design as dinner, tea, coffee and breakfast sets, and the exhibition toured the country for several months.

In its lifetime Harrods has mounted some extraordinary in-store exhibitions in the Central Hall on the ground floor. This area highlights the difference between the Knightsbridge store and its rivals: no one else would dare to devote 560 square metres/6,000 square feet of prime selling space in the heart of the shop to displays which aim to inform as much as to sell. Inspiration from abroad has produced some of the most striking displays. In 1990 an ice model of the Eiffel Tower formed part of a gourmet foods promotion featuring demonstrations by top chefs such as Albert Roux, Christian Guillut and Anton Edelmann. In autumn 1990 Harrods held its biggest promotion ever. Reflecting the fact that Italy supplies over ten per cent of the store's merchandise, 'A Grand Tour of Italy' featured different regions of Italy over five weeks.

## WINDOW DISPLAYS

Harrods window displays have been the envy of the trade for many years because of their sparse, elegant style. In marked contrast to the 'pile it high, sell it cheap' department stores, only a few products are featured in each of the eighty windows, which are changed every two to four weeks. Harrods was the first retailer to use temporary background scenery in window displays, in 1933, a lead that the whole of the trade has followed.

## CELEBRITY VISITS

Harrods has welcomed celebrities throughout its life, whether they are buying goods from the store, or helping to sell their own. Sports personalities such as golfer Henry Cotton have dispensed advice in the Sports department; Noel Coward and Oscar Peterson have tinkled the ivories of a Harrods piano; and the Books department has become a second home for many authors prepared to read from, or sign, their books. Enid Blyton read her works to enraptured children for three days in 1945, and signed 1,000 books. LP Hartley and Dame Margot Fonteyn have signed their works at the store. Joan Collins' book-signing session in 1988 attracted record crowds... and the only store in the world where Nancy Reagan was prepared to sign her autobiography was Harrods.

OPPOSITE: A special exhibition in 1934 allowed artists to try their hand at ceramic design. This plate is from a set by Laura Knight. Depicting scenes from the circus, her designs proved the most popular of all.

Noel Coward, shown here in 1933, was one of many celebrities
who played in the Harrods piano department.

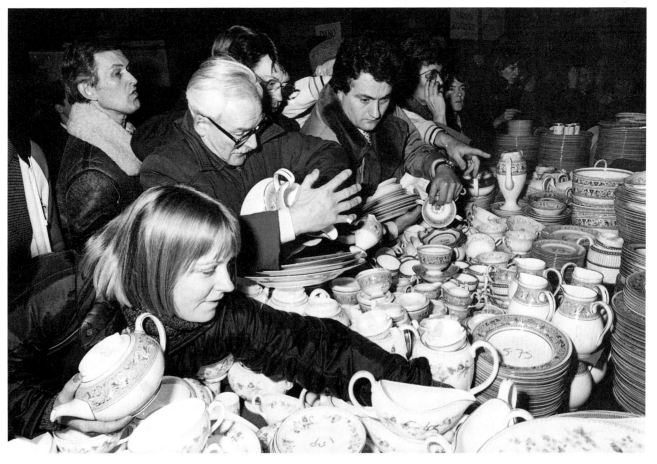

An image recognised across the world: Harrods' Sale inspires particular
pandemonium in the China department.

## THE HARRODS SALE

Twice a year Harrods sheds its decorum for its famous Sale. The frenetic
scenes it creates are in marked contrast to life at the store the rest of the
year. However, the customers of the 1990s are better prepared for the sale,
some even planning their route beforehand. With 300,000 customers on the
first day – nearly nine times the average figure of a normal day – the store
has been known to grind to a complete halt in a huge human traffic jam. A
member of staff commented of the atmosphere in the 1930s, 'It is the week
when even the sweetest-tempered have been known to snap and snarl,
when even more staunch friendships have been broken than ever before.'

It is not clear when the first Harrods Sale was held. In 1894 it
advertised a special sale of a job lot of wines bought at auction. It was still
running special sales of such acquisitions in 1914, when jewellery and silver
were on offer. But by 1910 the annual Harrods one-week sale was well-
established, for it was popular enough to merit the store's running special
trains to London from around the country, an idea Harrods pioneered.

For many years individual departments of the store ran separate sales at different times of the year. In 1935, for example, the White Sale in the Linen department was advertised with 985 light bulbs taking up 54 metres/176 feet of the frontage to spell out the date of the sale. The piano sale was famous too, and in that year its advertising carried endorsements from Henry Wood, Dr Malcolm Sargent and Sir Landon Ronald. In that sale one could get an upright piano for 15/-; the department was able to sell 100 pianos on the first day.

## A MASSIVE OPERATION

The Harrods Sale has always been an operation run on a massive scale. Back in 1929 the 1,500 extra staff helped in sales of 92 tons of sugar, 70 tons of soap and more than 5,000 tons of biscuits to take the turnover for the week to nearly half a million pounds. The Despatch department worked around the clock to make 204,000 deliveries within a five kilometre/three-mile radius of the store alone, contributing to a total of 493,000 deliveries resulting from the Sale. The bargain hunters were back in strength the following year, according to one staff account of the 1930 Sale:

> Half an hour before the time for opening, customers began to gather at every entrance, and at nine it reminded one of the opening of the gates at a football match. The customers knew where they wanted to go, and probably knew the bargain they wanted, and it was in many cases a lively sprint to get there.... In the afternoon the tea shops in the neighbourhood had to close their doors, so great was the flow of customers, an event unprecedented in the district in normal times.

That 'lively sprint' is the norm today – in 1988 bargain hunter Ian Birch, an accountant from Taunton, set a record of reaching the China department (on the second floor) in 13 seconds. That year film star Charlton Heston commented that the store at sale time was 'more crowded than the chariot race in Ben Hur'. Aptly, 1988 was also the year when the Toy department completely sold out of its miniature Rolls Royce children's cars – for the better class of rascal.

Part of the reason for the continuing crush is that Harrods advertises the event around the world, so that a sizeable number of people are aware of its slogan 'There is only one Harrods. There is only one Sale.' Recently it has begun to invite celebrities to open the proceedings – pop star Jason Donovan, and John Forsythe, star of the TV series 'Dynasty', have both helped to set the wheels of the first day in motion.

Today a countdown on short-wave radio ensures that all doors open simultaneously to let the excited crowds in. The first day, in particular, induces a kind of collective hysteria which numbs the brain. In 1983 a woman was so desperate to find a certain make of china that she dived under the table to pursue her quarry – and was unable to escape. It took

[160]

some time for staff to hear her cries and for security guards to clear sufficient space to allow her to crawl out, bedraggled and still plate-less. Such was the crush in one of the temporary fitting rooms the same year that a woman found herself unavoidably nudged and pushed back on to the shop floor. . . naked!

Staff also tell of an exhausted female bargain hunter who was seen to stagger with her armful of purchases into the gentlemen's toilets. After staring for several minutes at the security guard standing nonplussed in front of her, the woman enquired indignantly, 'Well, is this lift going up or down?'

Every year sees the record for turnover broken. A particular landmark came in 1984, when the Sale took turnover for the year to more than £200 million – the first time an individual British store had taken so much money in a full trading year. The January 1990 Sale achieved £45 million.

Work on the Sale starts months ahead, for 18,000 signs and tickets are beautifully hand-written, 500 extra tills installed, and 30 temporary fitting rooms put up on the first floor. Eighty windows are freshly dressed in the final five days before the big event commences. Weary staff wash down 30,000 biscuits with more than 7,400 litres/13,000 pints of orange juice during the Sale as they take a break from the frenzy of the shop floor. Meanwhile, every day the customers walk away having used up over a million litres/a quarter of a million gallons of the water from Harrods' own wells, and leaving thirteen tons of rubbish to be taken away.

Harrods is happy to take this kind of treatment: at the end of every Sale, 2.5 million carrier bags have left the store, their holders thoroughly delighted with the bargains inside.

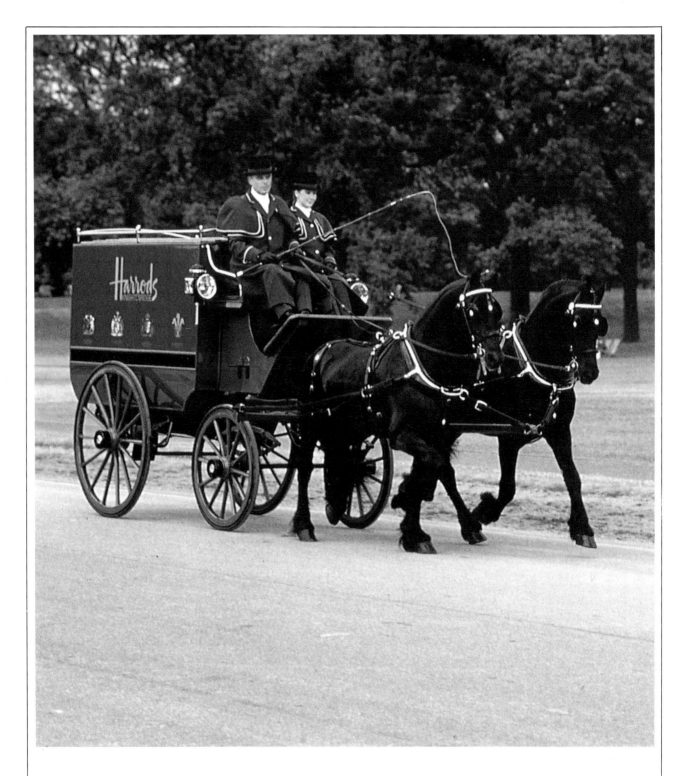

Magnificent black stallions pull a Harrods delivery cart
around Knightsbridge: the store of today aims to re-create
some of the excitement of its past.

CHAPTER NINE

# NEW FOUNDATIONS

———— *Harrods* ————

# "The Romance of Retailing"

The year 1985 was of special significance for the future of Harrods. The acquisition of the store by the Fayed family and its return to private ownership prompted a re-evaluation of the state of the Knightsbridge emporium, both physically and as a business.

Mohamed Al Fayed, the new chairman, was unhappy to see the effects of the seven-year battle to repel a hostile takeover bid. During the boardroom struggle, investment in the store had been neglected and the greatest jewel in the crown of the House of Fraser was sorely lacking in lustre. A bold hand and a sense of Harrods' history and tradition were badly needed. As so often is the case with British institutions, it took a fresh pair of eyes to recognise what needed to be done.

## A NEW PANACHE

The new Harrods chairman believes strongly that the essence of good retailing is excitement. He wants customers to feel that every visit is an occasion, and he deprecates those stores which take their customers for granted, opening their sales and other special events with no particular panache.

Now at Harrods celebrities previously welcomed as esteemed shoppers are invited to officially open the January and July Sales. Instead of simply opening up Santa's Grotto at Christmas as it did in the past, the store organises a Santa Claus Parade around the streets of Knightsbridge; the parade attracts thousands and signals the start of the capital's Christmas celebrations. Mr Fayed is a keen equestrian and has re-introduced the horse-drawn Harrods delivery vehicles that were once such a feature of

Knightsbridge life. Each of these small changes injects a measure of adrenalin into Harrods' blue-blooded veins.

But the rethink went much deeper. 'Harrods is a place steeped in tradition.' Mohamed Al Fayed explains. 'If you grew up as I did in a country where history is never far away, you constantly see the glory of old civilisation. Harrods is not just a money-making venture for me, it is part of Britain's heritage. It is a place which I love. Because I love it, I will ensure that it remains simply the most beautiful store in the world.'

It was in this spirit that 1987 saw the commencement of an extensive £250 million-plus programme of modernisation and regeneration with three key elements: refurbishment of certain departments to their splendid past elegance; expansion of some departments and indeed of the overall selling area; and the construction of a state-of-the-art warehouse in West London.

The restoration path had already been trodden to a degree in the magnificent Food Halls, but even here further improvements were made, notably with the new ceiling and chandeliers in the Floral Hall. Now other sections were given not so much a face-lift as major surgery, to re-create the elegance of the early twentieth century. Fittings and boardings were ripped away to reveal the hidden splendour of previous decorations. What could be kept was restored: what was past repair was re-created.

Some examples of the superb results can be seen in the Leather Room's green marble pillars and intricately worked art deco bronze grills, or the lush carpets and marble walkways and pillars of the Man's Shop. The Harrods Bank has been re-established in the basement, designed to meet the service requirements of the late twentieth century, but capturing the glory of its early years. The original architect's drawings were used for the bank's fixtures and fittings, and most customers think it dates from the Edwardian era rather than 1989. Departments still like to assert their own identity and so a number of architectural styles are celebrated through the decor of the ground floor. The elegant columns of the Palladian-style Fine Jewellery Room are a particularly fine example. Other areas of the store too were transformed, always with the aim not merely of restoring a look but of adding to the sense of tradition that is so fundamental to the Harrods persona.

## OPENING UP THE BASEMENT

Remarkably, more selling space was squeezed out of the existing building. It became apparent in the mid 1980s that about a fifth of the huge, sprawling building was unused, mainly due to the ad hoc nature of much of the previous building work. Now a comprehensive re-assessment has resulted not only in various departments moving to new parts of the building, but also the opening up of the fifth floor and, even more importantly, the basement for retail use. This initiative symbolises the new

The Egyptian Room, opening in 1991, represents a new era
for Harrods with its exotic decor and its escalator
opening up the basement to customers.

foundations that are being put in place to keep Harrods as a peak of
excellence for another 150 years.

The Egyptian Room, scheduled to open on the ground floor in
mid-1991, is inspired by the Alexandria homeland of the store's owners,
and represents the beginning of a new era at Harrods. Constructed in
granite and stone, it will be decorated with inlaid woods, paintings and
friezes in an authentic Egyptian style. High-quality merchandise orna-
mented in an Egyptian theme will be stocked throughout its 1,100 square
metres/12,000 square feet. The inspiration for much of the decor comes
from the 18th Dynasty (1580–1370 BC) which was a time of great artistic
freedom. The British Museum was called in for advice by the designer
seeking to satisfy the Chairman's insistence on authenticity. The Egyptian
Room will be flanked by the Room of Luxury and the Edwardian Room.

Perhaps most significant for the future of the store, an escalator will
lead down from the Egyptian Room to a walkway which is to run the
length of the building, finishing at the Harrods Bank. The designers have
opted to highlight the basement location with a stone floor, low ceiling and

The gates close on the long-serving Barnes depository, the
Harrods warehouse that belonged to the past.

wide decorated columns that look as if they are holding up the vast structure above. Various small shopping areas will be found on each side of this wide causeway. Adding 3,066 square metres/33,000 square feet of selling space, this venture marks the first time Harrods has sold goods from its basement, breaking an important barrier in the expansion of the store.

Moving from the depths to the heights of the building, the opening of the Sports and Leisure department on the fifth floor in February 1991 marked a victory for shoppers over administrators, as it involved ripping down office space to make room for a massive department where fashion and sportswear go hand in hand. Oak walkways link areas of patterned green carpet, reminiscent of a golf links, on which are stocked myriad items for the growing sports and leisure market. These initiatives in opening up the fortresses of the fifth floor and basement will take Harrods' total selling space to more than 93,000 square metres/one million square feet.

## NEW DEMANDS

Rather less glamorous, but equally indicative of Harrods' intent to stay at the top is the computerised distribution centre west of London at Osterley. The Old Barnes depository represented all that was good about Harrods early this century: a magnificent, imposing building staffed by innumerable dedicated staff who created a hurly-burly of urgent efficiency. But as the world has changed, so has retailing, and the buildings began to inflict major operational difficulties as the store strove to meet customers' ever more varied tastes. Many millions of items can be stored in the 18 metre/ 59 foot high computerised racking systems at Osterley, before being transported to the store or direct to customers by the new fleet of vans all equipped with cellular telephones.

## SIGNATURE SHOP

A few miles from Osterley is Heathrow airport, site of another key element in the future of the great store, the largest-yet Harrods shop outside Knightsbridge. This tax-free shop, covering 1,100 square metres/12,000 square feet, sells a range of Harrods 'signature' merchandise bearing the Harrods script, and is partnered by a 110 square metre/1,200 square foot Speciality Food Hall. The 'signature shop', which opened in the summer of 1990, marks a major advance in the spread of small Harrods 'signature shops' at airports around the world. Yet these are but satellites to the great establishment at Knightsbridge: there is only one Harrods, and there will always only be one Harrods.

The challenge the store is now facing is to ensure that Harrods remains the best store in the world, and not a museum to past glories. The improvements introduced after 1985 laid the foundations for further growth and greater responsiveness to retailing change, allowing the great store to remain a beacon of excellence, a palace of 'accessible exclusivity'.

An illustration from a Harrods promotional booklet of the Edwardian era, when the store supplied its customers with every possible requirement for Royal Ascot and other Society events. These gowns cost around $16\frac{1}{2}$ guineas, and the hats from 6 to $12\frac{1}{2}$ guineas.

# CHRONOLOGY

ILLUSTRATED WITH A RANGE OF MERCHANDISE
FROM THE 1929 HARRODS GENERAL
CATALOGUE.

**1800** Charles Henry Harrod is born.

**1834** Harrod branches out from his work as a miller to open up a wholesale tea business in east London.

**1849** He becomes involved in the grocery store of a struggling client, Philip Burden, at 8 Middle Queen's Buildings, Knightsbridge.

**1853** Harrod completes the takeover of Burden's shop. The area grows in prosperity and social cachet as London expands westwards.

**1861** He agrees to sell the business to one of his sons, Charles Digby Harrod, who has already served an apprenticeship at a shop in the City.

**1864** Charles Digby Harrod makes the final payment and moves into the rooms above the shop. He bans credit and cuts his prices – bold moves for a modest grocer in a still very mixed area.

**1873** As the business grows, an extension is built over the back garden.

**1874** The name 'Harrod's Stores' appears for the first time on the windows.

**1880** Harrod introduces own-label groceries.

**1883** On 6 December fire completely destroys the premises, which are bulging with Christmas goods. Harrod rents a local building and meets every order, capturing the public imagination with his determination to overcome his adversity.

**1884** New, larger premises open on the same site, with an increased range of goods on sale on two floors.

**1885** Charles Henry Harrod dies.

**1889** Charles Digby Harrod sells his now flourishing grocery business, for £120,000 cash, and it is formed into a limited company. Deprived of his eagle-eyed management, the store goes into decline.

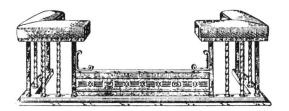

**1891** After two years during which trade has suffered badly, Richard Burbidge is appointed general manager. He has built up a fine reputation from stints at other stores, including the larger rival Whiteleys. Under him, Harrods grows physically and by reputation into a national institution – and before the turn of the century overtakes his past employer's store as the best in London.

**1893** Richard Burbidge's son Woodman starts work at the shop.

**1894** In one of a number of property deals, Harrods purchases an old soap factory in Barnes which is to become a depository.

**1897** Richard Burbidge makes significant progress in expanding the store by acquiring the leases of neighbouring shops, a pub and a school, as he endeavours to take over a complete 4.5 acre island site.

**1898** Amid much public excitement, Harrods unveils its 'moving staircase' – London's first escalator.

**1901** More property deals enlarge the site, and work begins on the modern facade.

**1909** Harrods celebrates the sixtieth anniversary of its founding (though 1849 is more likely to have been the year in which Charles Henry Harrod became involved in Philip Burden's shop).

**1911** With a final flurry of lease purchases, the whole island site is finally acquired.

**1913** Queen Mary awards the store a Royal Warrant of Appointment. Harrods opens a shop in Buenos Aires (later sold).

**1914** During World War I, 2,000 Harrods staff enter the services, and the store builds and equips Belgian hospitals. Harrods buys Dickins & Jones, Regent Street.

**1916** Richard Burbidge is made a Baronet.

**1917** Sir Richard dies, and is succeeded by his son Woodman as managing director.

**1920** Richard Burbidge ('Mr Richard'), Sir Woodman's son, joins the firm.

**1921** Sir Woodman becomes chairman after death of Sir Alfred Newton.

**1924** Second-floor flats are converted into sales areas.

**1927** Third-floor flats join them.

**1935** Sir Woodman retires from managing directorship but remains chairman. He is succeeded by his son Richard.

**1939** Windows are boarded up as World War II commences and air raids are threatened.

**1945** Sir Woodman dies. His son Sir Richard takes over as chairman.

**1949** Major celebrations are held for the store's centenary year.

**1959** Scottish store group House of Fraser wins a three-cornered take-over battle for the now eight-store Harrods Group amid much public speculation.

**1966** Lord Fraser dies, and is succeeded as chairman by his son, Sir Hugh Fraser.

**1967** Harrods launches Way In, an in-store boutique designed to appeal to younger customers.

**1970** Robert Midgley is appointed managing director, and spends a decade updating the store, transforming it in many ways into the establishment it is today.

**1974** Bomb explodes in store; no one is injured.

**1980** Aleck Craddock becomes managing director. Large scale refurbishment (Harrods Major Project) commences, including refurbishment of Food Halls and the creation of more selling space.

**1981** Sir Hugh Fraser is deposed as chairman of the group by Professor Roland Smith.

**1983** IRA car bomb kills six people and injures ninety-three.

**1984** 'Tiny' Rowland of Lonrho, having failed in take-over bid for the group, sells his shares to Mohamed Al Fayed.

**1985** Mohamed Al Fayed buys the whole group for £615 million, and takes it into private ownership. Under him Harrods begins a new and massive refurbishment and expansion programme, with the stated aim of recreating the elegant opulence of the store's Edwardian days.

**1990** Store begins trading from its fifth floor with the new Olympic Way sports complex, while also opening up basement areas as sales space. Harrods employs 4,000 staff working in 300 departments, and is established as the largest store in Europe, probably the largest in the world – and certainly the best-known.

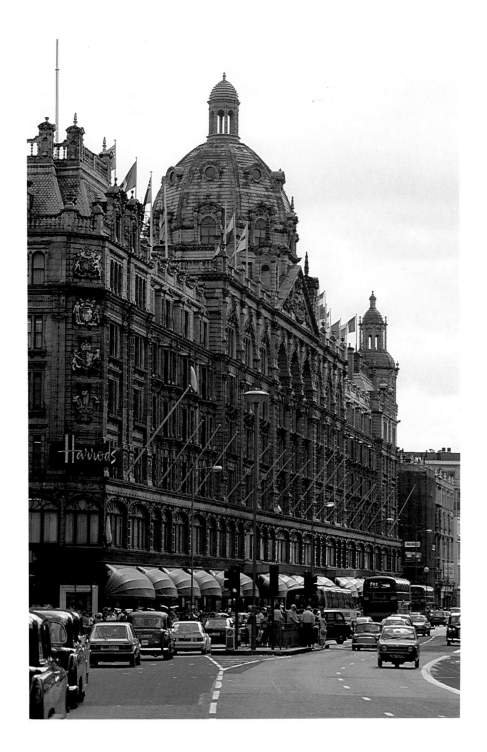

Visited by around 35,000 customers a day,
Harrods remains in a class of its own.

# INDEX

PICTURE CREDITS

The publishers wish to thank the following for their permission to reproduce photographs: the *Daily Express* (p 18), *Financial Times* (p 159), Hulton Picture Company (pp 77, 86), Ian Jones (pp 55 left, 59, 60 bottom left and right, 65 top and bottom right), Museum of London (pp 28, 34), National Portrait Gallery, London (pp 36, 37), Press Association (pp 139, 153), Rex Features (pp 10, 22), Robert Harding Picture Library (pp 44–5), Royal Commission Historic Monuments (pp 61, 119, 124), Jon Stewart (pp 46, 88, 161), Susan Griggs Agency (p 173) and Harrods' Archives (all other illustrations).